Guest Curator

Bruce W. Ferguson

Essays

Jean-Christophe Ammann

Donald B. Kuspit

Bruce W. Ferguson

Mendel Art Gallery

Saskatoon, Canada

Published for the exhibition *Eric Fischl: Paintings* by the Mendel Art Gallery, a nonprofit organization supported by donations and grants from the City of Saskatoon, Province of Saskatchewan, Saskatchewan Arts Board, The Canada Council, and Museum Assistance Programmes of the National Museums of Canada.

Photography:
Catalogue no. 1, 3, 4, 13, 14, 15— courtesy of the lenders
Catalogue no. 2, 7, 8 — Zindman/Fremont, New York, New York, U.S.A.
Catalogue no. 5 — Thomas Moore, Toronto, Ontario, Canada
Catalogue no. 6, 12 — courtesy of the Sable-Castelli Gallery, Toronto, Ontario, Canada
Catalogue no. 9 — the Cincinnati Art Museum, Cincinnati, Ohio, U.S.A.
Catalogue no. 10, 11 — courtesy of the Larry Gagosian Gallery, Los Angeles, California, U.S.A.
Catalogue no. 16, 17, 18, 20, 21 — Zindman/Fremont, courtesy of the Mary Boone Gallery, New York, New York, U.S.A.
Figure no. 1, 2, 5, 12 — Zindman/Fremont, courtesy of the Mary Boone Gallery, New York, New York, U.S.A.
Figure no. 3, 4 — Zindman/Fremont, courtesy of the Edward Thorp Gallery, New York, New York, U.S.A.
Figure no. 13 — courtesy of the Museum of Modern Art, New York, New York, U.S.A.

Design: McKay Goettler Design, Saskatoon
Printer: Houghton Boston, Saskatoon

Mendel Art Gallery
950 Spadina Crescent East
P.O. Box 569
Saskatoon, Saskatchewan, Canada S7K 3L6
(306) 664-9610

ISBN: 0-919863-14-0

ERIC FISCHL: PAINTINGS

WHITNEY MUSEUM OF AMERICAN ART
February 18–May 11, 1986

CHECKLIST OF ADDITIONAL PAINTINGS

This exhibition was organized for the Mendel Art Gallery, Saskatoon, Canada, by Bruce Ferguson.
It was installed, with some additional works, at the Whitney Museum by David Whitney.
All measurements are in inches, height precedes width.
All works are oil on canvas.

22. *Time for Bed*
1980
72 × 96
The Saatchi Collection
London, England

23. *Bad Boy*
1981
66 × 96
The Saatchi Collection
London, England

24. *Boy Oh Boy*
1982
66 × 96
Collection of the artist

25. *Birthday Boy*
1983
84 × 108
Collection of Maramotti, Albinea, Reggio Emilia, Italy

26. *A Visit To/A Visit From/The Island*
1983
84 × 168
Whitney Museum of American Art, New York;
Purchase, with funds from the Louis and Bessie Adler
Foundation, Inc., Seymour M. Klein, President

27. *Vanity*
1984
108 × 96
Collection of Michael S. Ovitz

28. *A Brief History of North Africa*
1985
88 × 120
Private collection, courtesy of Mary Boone Gallery
New York

This exhibition is supported by grants from Charles Simon and an Anonymous Donor.

Itinerary

Mendel Art Gallery
Saskatoon, Saskatchewan, Canada
8 February - 17 March 1985

Stedelijk Van Abbemuseum
Eindhoven, The Netherlands
6 April - 5 May 1985

Kunsthalle Basel
Basel, Switzerland
12 May - 24 June 1985

Institute of Contemporary Arts
London, England
15 July - 21 August 1985

Art Gallery of Ontario
Toronto, Ontario, Canada
21 September - 3 November 1985

Museum of Contemporary Art
Chicago, Illinois, U.S.A.
22 November 1985 - 2 February 1986

The Broida Museum
New York, New York, U.S.A.
22 February - 29 March 1986

The following works will not be shown at every exhibition center:
Cat. 8 *Overnight*
Cat. 10 *Barbeque*
Cat. 19 *Saviour Mother, Save Your Love(r)*
Cat. 20 *Sisters*

Lenders to the Exhibition

Alcan Smelters and Chemicals Ltd.
The Artist, courtesy of Mary Boone Gallery
Mr. Douglas S. Cramer
The Downe Collection
Dr. and Mrs. Cecil Gilbert
Mr. Peter N. Greenwald
Robert and Doris Hillman
Mr. and Mrs. Aron B. Katz
Lonti Ebers Fine Arts Inc.
Mr. Barry Lowen
Lewis and Susan Manilow
The Menil Foundation
Tom and Charlotte Newby
Private Collections
RSM Company
The Saatchi Collection
Sable-Castelli Gallery Ltd.
Mr. Martin Sklar
The Smorgon Family Contemporary American Art Collection
The Speyer Family Collection

14. *The Sheer Weight of History*
1982
152 x 152
The Downe Collection
New York, New York, U.S.A.

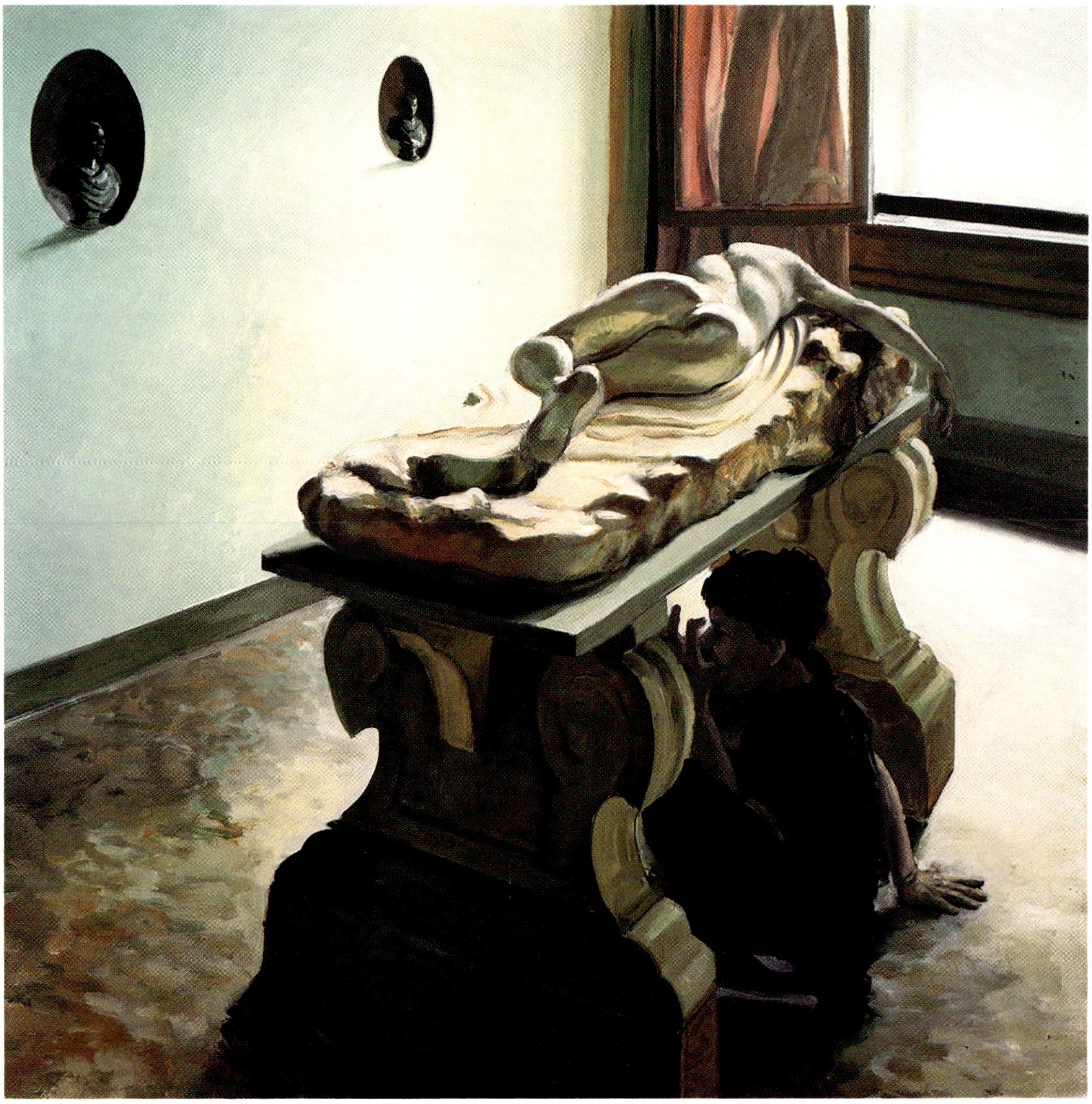

Foreword

The large, figurative paintings of New York artist Eric Fischl are decidedly aggressive and deliberately confrontational. His depictions of the suburban leisured existence of the American upper middle class, in all of its nakedness (both symbolic and real), hover between dream-like fiction and mundane truth. Central to their success is the unavoidable involvement demanded by the otherwise passive viewer, who is suddenly a voyeur of intimate scenes and an unwilling actor in the narrative. There is a psychological complicity among artist, subject and viewer (referred to by one critic as a conspiracy) which has been intentionally constructed. It is not surprising then that as viewers we may react to Fischl's paintings with varying degrees of anxiety. We are at once provoked yet fascinated, seduced yet repelled.

In this sense, Fischl's paintings straddle a line between nineteenth century historical precedent and contemporary reinterpretation of figurative content. One imagines, for example, that we receive Fischl's images in much the same way as Edouard Manet's contemporaries responded to his provocative paintings over one hundred years ago. And as was true for Manet, the power of Fischl's art is not wholly resident in the content of the images themselves. The studied craftsmanship with which Eric Fischl renders his subjects is key. Skin, water, and artificial or natural light are as skillfully manipulated in paint as the audience is in spirit. Fischl's handling of the material is masterful.

Eric Fischl lives and works in New York City. His first solo exhibition was in Canada, at the Dalhousie Art Gallery, Halifax, when the artist was an instructor at the Nova Scotia College of Art and Design. He was a colleague there of Allan MacKay, my predecessor as curator-director of the Mendel Art Gallery, on whose initiative this exhibition was organized. Now, ten years after the artist's first Canadian exhibition, the Mendel Art Gallery in Saskatoon is honored to mount this major exhibition which will circulate to The Netherlands, Switzerland, England, Ontario and the United States after its Saskatoon showing.

Many individuals and organizations have assisted the Mendel Art Gallery with this project, and they are acknowledged here with gratitude. Thanks are expressed first to the artist, Eric Fischl, on whose willing cooperation and patient sense of humor we have depended for the past two years. We hope he is pleased with the results. The artist's dealer, Mary Boone of Mary Boone Gallery, New York, and her staff assisted the Gallery in numerous practical ways and we are grateful for their commitment and cooperation. Thanks are also due to Eric Fischl's former dealer, Edward Thorp of the Edward Thorp Gallery, New York, who extended generous assistance in the early stages of planning this exhibition. The lenders to the exhibition, who are listed elsewhere in this catalogue, deserve the Gallery's very special thanks. We warmly appreciate their generosity in agreeing to part with their paintings for an extended period of time in order to share them with a wide, international audience. We also appreciate the work of the contributors to this exhibition catalogue: Jean-Christophe Ammann is Director of the Kunsthalle Basel in Switzerland, and Donald Kuspit is an art critic working out of New York.

Finally, Bruce Ferguson, independent curator and art critic from Montreal, whose responsibilities as guest curator of *Eric Fischl: Paintings* included the selection of the work and the contribution of an essay, has organized an exhibition of which the Gallery and the artist can be truly proud. It has been a pleasure to work with him.

Linda Milrod
Curator-Director

Funding assistance from The Canada Council and the Saskatchewan Arts Board is acknowledged with gratitude.

Eric Fischl's View: To Whom Does It Belong?

Jean-Christophe Ammann

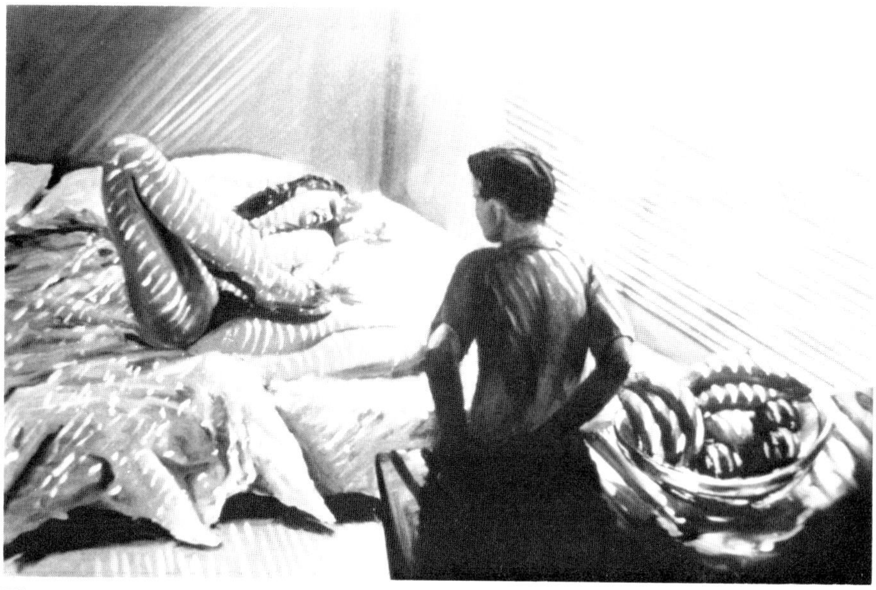

Fig. 1. *Bad Boy* 1981

Eric Fischl is not unknown to audiences in Europe. As early as 1978 the Kunsthalle Basel presented his work on the occasion of a group exhibition of some Canadian artists, *Neun Kanadische Künstler.* His participation resulted from a longer stay in Halifax, Nova Scotia. At that time his paintings were still more like picture-objects: metaphors for the modes of existence and modes of communication of the peninsula's inhabitants, fishermen for the most part, whose perilous way of life, mission in life and life rhythm he not only observed, but rather uncovered, layer by layer. When, during the same year (1978), Fischl moved to New York, he began to translate his view of the reality surrounding him into oil on canvas, mostly in the form of self-contained picture-details, in which, however, the prerequisites were now different inasmuch as, in accordance with his new habitat, he took his motifs from American middle-class everyday life, from the treadmill of weekends spent with the family, and from the more or less intimate hours during the course of the day.

Fischl's eye for and perspective of the reality broadly surrounding him has always something to do with discovering. This becomes clearly evident in his viewpoint, that is, in the manner in which he selects the detail of the picture or in his composition: as if one unexpectedly entered a room, as if one were looking from above through a window (*Aufsicht,* view from above) or through a window (*Durchblick,* through-view), as if one were sitting a little off to the side in a beach chair and, glancing up from a book, contemplating what was going on (*Untersicht,* view from below), as if one suddenly became aware of a situation in passing, as if one unexpectedly became witness to an event.

Here the question immediately arises: Who is "one"? The answer, "the artist of course," hardly gets one further. For the view of the artist, a different one altogether, shifts to a perception in which knowledge and experience do not as yet correspond with each other. I am of the opinion, therefore, that it is the view of a boy, a boy who has just recently reached puberty, who apprehends the grown-up world, but also his world, in the intermediate domain of erotic ambiguity. *How* he sees this world, and to a lesser extent what he sees, is what is crucial. Through his manner of seeing, the often altogether usual becomes specific to such a degree that the viewer of the painting, who almost inevitably adopts the perspective of the viewer substituted by the artist, is, in a subversive way, forced to adopt this manner of seeing.

While the viewer does this he simultaneously — knowingly and yet unknowingly — becomes the viewer of his own viewing of the painting, thus activating his memory in the direction of something comparably experienced. It is precisely this viewpoint that Eric Fischl adopts in certain paintings when, so to speak, he portrays the viewer dissociated as the one viewing. For example, in *Bad Boy* 1981 (Fig. 1), the boy, just entering a bedroom (view from the back), intensely contemplates a naked woman who, while dreaming (?), stretches lasciviously (his mother?). From this *Bad Boy* results a *Birthday Boy* 1983 (Fig. 2) who, with propped-up arm, pensively gazes into the straddled thighs of a woman lying beside him. And in *Sleepwalker* 1979 (Cat.1), the viewer captures the bent silhouette of a masturbating boy in a child's swimming pool.

Qualifying the discovering manner of seeing defines painting. Painting is sub-

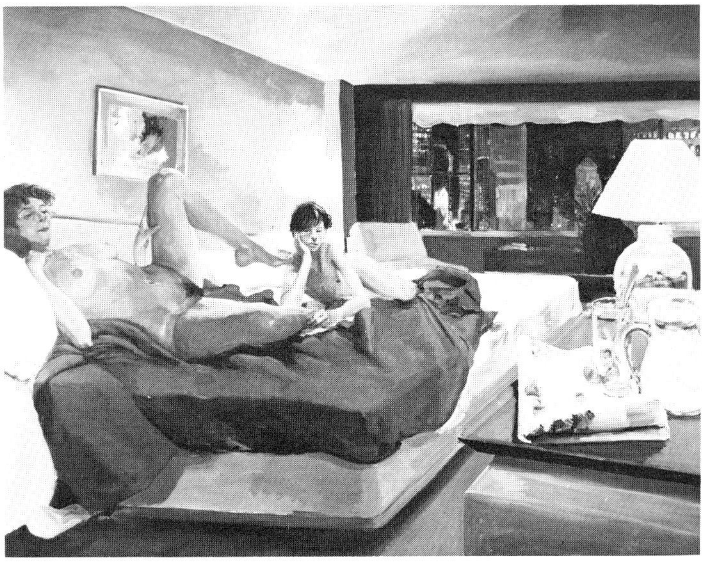

Fig. 2. *Birthday Boy* 1983

ordinate to the manner of seeing to the extent that it embodies the atmospherical element of the event taking place in the distance between the viewer and the event as the event itself. (In sculpture comparable to the *Diego* portraits by Alberto Giacometti.) To emphasize this seems important to me because we are not dealing here with the problems of realistic portrayal.

Fischl variously clarifies the manner of seeing in the combination of several self-contained viewpoints, as in *Inside Out* (Fig. 3) and *Dog Days* (Cat. 18) both 1983, and in the sense of possible simultaneity or temporally different moments.

In *Dog Days* there are two temporally different moments, because the location of the event is the same (scene of a balcony with a view to the street and sea). On the panel to the left a naked woman with a beachbag, in the presence of two attentive dogs, leaves the house to go swimming. Taking advantage of the absence of this woman, in the panel to the right, an excited boy, standing,

prim American realism from photorealism to Pearlstein where a pseudo-vacuousness masks the voyeuristic obsession — helps the implication. But if one looks at what the protagonists in his compressed narrative dramas are doing — compressed to the point of seeming to implode, as in *Best Western* (Cat. 16) and *Master Bedroom* (Cat. 17) both 1983, with their sharply reduced casts, a single figure in cameo self-sufficiency,

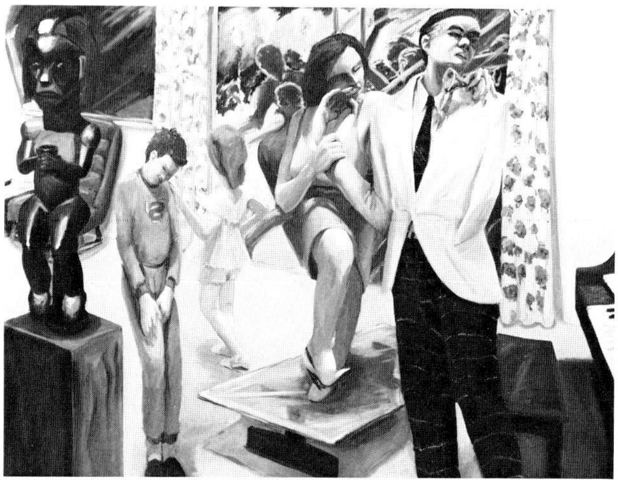

Fig. 4. *Time for Bed* 1980

immediately identifiable because the role-player and the real person seamlessly fuse — there is nothing actually untoward or even unseemly occurring, at least nothing in these enlightened times that is unexpected. There's nothing out of the ordinary, unimagined, in seeing a solitary boy masturbate, as in *Sleepwalker* 1979 (Cat. 1): what else is one to do with one's solitude in America? Why else does one want to be alone in the modern world? Whether a solitary or public person, like the boy with the hots in *Time for Bed* 1980 (Fig. 4), what else is the American but a mechanical performer, almost banally selfless?

The words in this essay's epigraph are those of Ellison's invisible black man, recollecting an event of his boyhood, when, along with other black youths, he was exposed to the delights of a naked white woman — an impossible situation which he did not expect to come out of alive. He is allowed to look but not touch, and the "wave of irrational guilt and fear" and violence he feels follows from this condition, as well as from the lynching threat. He "was strongly attracted and looked in spite of" himself. He would have looked "had the price of looking been blindness." His "eyes brushed slowly over her body": his looking is unrushed, complex, despite the danger of the situation, the danger of looking. It is unrushed because there is no other sensing but looking. The erotic encounter is confined to looking and fraught with the threat of death, which escalates the tension almost unbearably. Also, the naked woman looked at, observed with an intensity that makes observation an act of participation in her body, is mature and physically ripe, especially in comparison to the boy, and loaded down with symbolic meaning. This is a freight she easily carries by reason of the artifice of her glamor as well as the real sumptuousness of her body, and by the excitement it arouses both in the boy and the onlookers who staged the scene — the big shot white men of the small town, who drunkenly begin to riot and chase the woman, naked as she is, into the street. Her naked body acquires symbolic power not only because the burden of its reality presses down on the boy, because its reality is experienced as a burden by him, but because it is equipped, at a strategic place, with a small American flag. This tattoo serves less as a fig leaf than as a marker and pointer, as effective as any billboard sign, of a very important place, the arena of gratification.

Is it possible to say that by reason of the flag she becomes the bitch goddess of success whom William James said Americans worshipped, and that the black youth is confronted with something he cannot possess — something he can only look at but not touch? This is what makes his situation particularly excruciating, as though its death-predicated sexual character was only a launching pad for a deeper frustration, an announcement of an even more desperate despair, because based on a more absolute — irremediable — situation. The youth may eventually, if he survives this situation (as he does), have his sex, even with such a woman (as he does), but he will never have success, even be allowed as near to it as he was to the white woman. This is partly why he goes underground, decides to be deliberately "invisible": he consciously chooses the invisibility which others conferred on him because he was born black.

Now all this anguish, this melodramatic tension, this provocation and exploitation of irrational feelings, the symbolic implications, as well as the real perversity of the youth's situation, are absent from Fischl's pictures, or at least not clearly signaled. Indeed, Ellison's story is not a middle-class American story, a story of what other-directed Americans do with their leisure life, as Fischl's stories are. Ellison's youth is as "un-American" in his terror as the African fetish object on the television set in the room where Fischl's adolescents have their *Slumber Party* 1983 (Fig. 5), or in the room depicted in *Time For Bed*, where the party seems just about to really begin rather than come to an end. The terror of Ellison's youth is inappropriate except when, as in the African statue, it can be frozen into decorative status, neutralized into an environmental nicety, for all the statue's implied significance in the situation —for all the unconscious undertow it focuses through its savage demonstrativeness. But that's just the point: the perverse must be kept in an uncertain connotative limbo in Fischl,

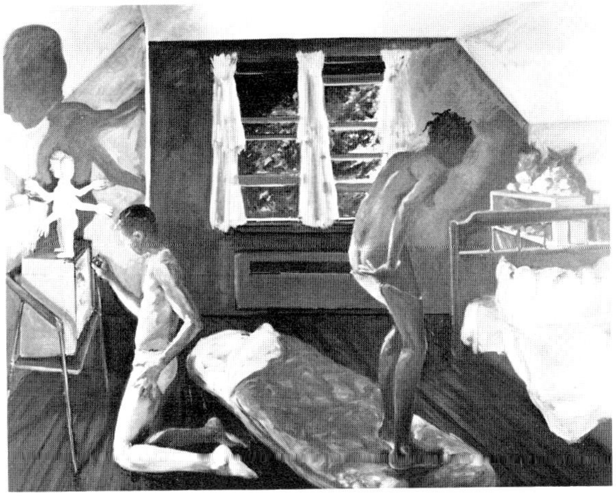

Fig. 5. *Slumber Party* 1983

just as the sexuality, for all its explicitness, as in *Dog Days* 1983 (Cat. 18), seems peculiarly invalid, vapid, inarticulate, even inchoate. Yes, the boy has an erection and is touching the girl on the white skin left behind by the panties of her bikini bathing suit — just where the tattooed American flag was on Ellison's voluptuous white woman — but the whole event seems rather inconsequential, as inconsequential as the mating of the two dogs in the adjoining panel. Indeed, the juxtaposition of the two panels not only sets up a system of interchangeable surrogates, but the adolescents could as easily be transformed dogs as the dogs mutant adolescents.

The coimplication is complete in Fischl, a strategy of parallelism — also operational in *Time for Bed,* where the children can be said to emulate the adults, but also vice versa — which neutralizes both sides of its equation, confirming the aura of inconsequence already mediated by the everyday environment in which the event is embedded. The boy's arousal in *Dog Days* hardly seems important, and the panoramic outdoors space in which Fischl sets his erection dwindles its size. Indeed, we almost overlook it. The use of covertly grand space to undermine significance by cutting the scenic contents down to manageable size is another strategy of the neutralization or cooling of potentially hot contents that Fischl uses. 'Covertly,' because the grand space is often sectioned by the objects that echo it, especially the king-size beds in *Birthday Boy* 1983 (Fig. 2), *Master Bedroom,* and an *Untitled (Two Women in Bedroom)* 1982 (Cat. 15) picture of two naked women. The depicting of supposedly private space, such as balconies, bedrooms, in such a grand manner, makes it continuous with public space. Indeed, it often is public space — the bedrooms are often motel rooms — put to private use, which in fact is a publicly known and sanctioned use. "What goes on behind closed doors" is hardly private in the modern, enlightened world.

In this context it is worth noting that there is still another strategy Fischl uses to cool down his potentially hot scenes, a less obvious but nonetheless subtly effective one. Fischl's *Master Bedroom* reminds one of Oldenburg's motel bedroom ensemble, both in its bizarre perspective and pointless, seemingly infinitely expandable openness, although not in its tacky textures. Similarly, *The Old Man's Boat and the Old Man's Dog* 1982 (Cat. 11) reminds one of Hemingway, in however distorted a way; *Overnight* 1981 (Cat. 8) echoes Schiele's *Family; New House* 1982 (Cat. 13) is a Hopperesque scene of loneliness or desertion; Courbet's *Funeral at Ornans* sprang to mind when I saw *A Funeral* 1980 (Cat. 2); and *Catch* 1981 (not illustrated) has a Reginald Marsh-like dimension. The strategy here is what I would call neutralization through art historical parallelism. It is not so much a matter of allusion to past accomplishments to buttress and justify Fischl's present effort, to give it unexpected depth, but of setting the banal present scene in a grand context, to uphold its banality, thus managing it so that it does not become as unruly as it might become. The art historical and literary allusions help remind us that whatever else it might be the scene is above all staged, manipulated, contrived, totally artificial. This recognition, deviously forcing itself upon us, prevents an expressionistic response to it, a response like that of Ellison's boy. Nothing really taboo-breaking is at stake. Staginess of form displaces inherent perversity of content as the heart of fiction, and conveys its purpose of neutralization.

In *Dog Days* the adolescent boy touches the adolescent flesh of his girlfriend, completing perception. In Manet's *Olympia* the viewer is forced into the private space of the prostitute not only by her imperious if indifferent glance, but by the potential, easily realized for a sum of money, for touching her, possessing her. All of this touching and touching-to-come hardly has the potent charge of the untouchability of the white woman in Ellison's story — the castration of looking, by refusing to allow it to become erect touching, forced upon Ellison's youth. He is an involuntary eunuch, yet far from neutralized, cool. In contrast, Fischl's *Birthday Boy*, in his idealized viewer's position, is gratified simply by looking at the naked woman, which is hardly taboo. Nothing is in the enlightened modern world, which has put everything on view. He might as well be looking at a television screen, as the boy in *Slumber Party* does, after his sexual adventure with his girlfriend. The moment of consummation is missing in these pictures; frustration is not excessive. For all the physical intimacy involved, for all the implication of sinister passion, the events depicted are levelled by their voyeuristic meaning.

Fischl's pictures have been generally understood, in a Barthesean way, as nonlinear texts implicating the viewer in an "unfixed plurality" of meanings. They are a structure of signifiers belonging to different narrative networks rather than a structure of signifieds issuing in univocal meaning. Yet the networks of Fischl's neo-narrative seem to converge in a single story, as is evidenced by the fact that the majority of the protagonists are children on the verge of adolescence or already adolescent. Sometimes the child is almost secreted in the picture, as in *The Old Man's Boat and the Old Man's Dog*, where he is almost lost in the middle distance. But more often the child is upfront, the major actor, as in *Barbeque* 1982 (Cat. 10), *Sleepwalker, Best Western,* and *The Sheer Weight of History* 1982 (Cat. 14). When not the child's then the adult world as it might be seen from a childlike perspective, through the eyes of adolescent self-interest, is presented, as in *Sisters* 1984 (Cat. 20) and *Catch*, as well as the *Untitled* picture of two naked women. The view is from below, or strangely outside, in a context of idealized obliqueness. In *Untitled* we have essentially the same view as the *Birthday Boy* does. Fischl offers us adultomorphic pictures of an adolescent child's point of view, where the child is about to take up adult interests, perhaps already involved in what are usually thought of as adult (sexual) activities, but not fully in charge of their value, not fully knowing their worth as independent activities. He engages in them because they seem there to be engaged in, but his estimate of them is unclear. For all his erotic activity, his relationship to eros is still voyeuristic, peculiarly passive if not disengaged. The dispassionate air that hovers over the works confirms their voyeuristic involution, while forcefully objectifying them.

Heinz Kohut argues that the "perverse" voyeuristic activities "in which the child engages are . . . attempts to reestablish the union with the narcissistically invested lost object through visual fusion." [1] This narcissistically invested lost object is customarily the parent, with which the maturing child — the adolescent — can no longer merge, not only because it is socially forbidden but because it is maturationally inappropriate, passé. Fischl frequently shows us adolescents eager to merge with one another through sexual activity, even sometimes mirroring each other physically, apart from their sexual difference — *Dog Days* is a prime example — but with the merger incomplete, bogged down in voyeuristic merging through looking or touching. Nor does Fischl show many examples of successful merging in the adult world, where there are many instances of isolation, as in *New House,* and hermetic insularity of feeling or psyche, as in *Grief* (Cat. 9) and *A Woman Possessed* (Cat. 6), both 1981. To overcome this threatening limbo between parental and erotic mergers — different ways of relating to the adult world with some narcissistic satisfaction — the adolescent needs a "transitional object" that he feels can be controlled simply through looking. Perceiving it in voyeuristic fixation one merges with it in a narcissistically satisfactory way. As has been said, "the basic perversion is fetishism . . . all other forms can be conceptually reduced to variations on the theme of manipulating an infantile fetish."[2] Voyeuristic looking is not only a way of manipulating an infantile fetish, but of creating one, of turning the object of one's perception into one. To establish a fetishistic relationship to an object is to merge narcissistically with and be satisfied by it. The African fetish objects already mentioned are far from accidental accompaniments to upper-middle-class daily life in Fischl's pictures. But the televisions which frequent his pictures are the most narcissistically satisfying, most infantile fetishes, because complete merger can be effected with them, simply through voyeuristic looking, which they encourage.

Narcissistically satisfying merger is possible through projected orgy, as in *Catch,* or through projected incest, as in *Father and Son Sleeping* 1980 (Cat. 5), and perhaps in *Birthday Boy* and in similar works where an adolescent boy voyeuristically views a woman's genitals and naked body up close. Of course, the perversion is implied rather than actually rendered — part of the coolness, the neutralization effect noted earlier — and may be nowhere near occurring. The physical intimacy may simply be part of the sportive liberalism of American leisure time activities, an allowable transgression during a quasi-Dionysian time of self-forgetfulness. But the real point is not the nakedness but that it symbolizes the voyeurism — its consummate, profoundly gratifying character. What in effect happens in the voyeuristic transaction is not only that the two become one through the looking of the less adult one, who thus regresses to an infantile ideal of merger, but that this oneness is established through the fetishizing of the adult. In effect, the empty lawn chairs of the parents in *Sleepwalker* are filled by the fetishized other. The big naked women are parents whether they want to be or not. They are not simply prostitutes who are hired to initiate the adolescent into the mystery of sex between their legs, who are made emphatic through their nakedness, but mothers with whom the adolescent can merge. They remain more satisfactory in their voyeuristic/fetishistic role than if the relationship was actually consummated sexually. Thus the implication of perversion permits the fetishizing voyeurism — the most fundamental perversion — to remain intact, undisturbed, quietly in play. Fischl never changes gear in any of his pictures, which are in voyeuristic overdrive, steadily unfolding a narrative of fetishism. Even in such pictures as *Christian Retreat* 1980 (Cat. 3) and *The Visit II* 1981 (Cat. 7), the voyeuristic view from outside (above) has its narcissistic value, since it permits the adolescent to witness places and scenes of adult revelry or relaxation — sex conceived as a relaxer rather than intensifier is particularly American, pragmatic — without literally joining in, thus preserving his infantile integrity. At the same time, an outsider perspective always makes insider activities seem more significant than they are, that is, more subject to fetishization, which is one way of getting narcissistic satisfaction out of them, of merging with them.

One last point should be made about

the psychodynamics of Fischl's pictures. From a Kleinean point of view, they can be understood not only as synthesizing the paranoid and depressive attitudes, but as being reparative. According to Melanie Klein, the child's life moves between the poles of paranoid and depressive anxiety. In the "paranoid position," the child suffers "fear of a massive and deadly retaliation by the mother's and the father's penis (inside the mother), revenging the destruction that the child has effected, in his fantasy, on the parents, particularly on their sexual union." Is *Birthday Boy* looking for the universal penis? Depressive anxiety articulates the "horror and dread concerning the fate of the whole object (the parent) whom the child fears he had destroyed." From this follow "attempts to save the love object, to repair and restore it."[3] Generally speaking, there is almost always one member of the parental pair missing in Fischl's pictures, an effect which I think powerfully contributes to their aura of suspended (rather than imminent) activity, their air of suspense. Where is the father in *Birthday Boy*? Where is the mother in *Father and Son Sleeping* or in *Barbeque*? Where are the naked adult men to match the naked adult women in *Sisters* and the *Untitled* image of two women? And when there is no missing or destroyed parent, familial membership is so blurred, as in *Catch* and *The Old Man's Boat and the Old Man's Dog*, as to imply the meaninglessness of the family in the anonymous adult world. There we are all supposedly on our own, with only our narcissism to defend and sustain us — our voyeurism to give us perverse distance from the world, distance that is paradoxically at once infantile and philosophical, regressive and the root of contemplative understanding. This "meaninglessness" is perhaps the most effective fantasy destruction there can be.

At the same time that Fischl shows us the destruction of family unity in the infantile mind, especially the destruction of sexual union through perverse voyeuristic union, he shows us the tentative, no doubt ineffective, yet not entirely superficial restoration or reparation of family unity, in however ironical, even satirical, a form. The pet dogs that tend to proliferate in Fischl's pictures are the key to this. Where they are, the empathy of family existence is restored, fantasy destructiveness and anxiety are overcome through constructive unity with the highly personalized family pet. The girl in the *Master Bedroom* probably feels more for the dog she embraces than she ever will for the man she eventually will embrace, for the pet cares for her as strongly as she cares for it. They form a loving pair, a parental unit: the opposite of the empty parental unity implied by the two empty chairs in *Sleepwalker*. Similarly, the dog in *The Old Man's Boat and the Old Man's Dog* makes the scene familial as much as anonymously orgiastic, and the dogs in *Woman Surrounded by Dogs* 1980 (Cat. 4) are the woman's family. Jan van Eyck's *Arnolfini Marriage* and Georges Seurat's *Grande Jatte* have taught us that the pet dog ambiguously signifies fidelity and lust, perhaps fidelity through lust.

But this art historical background goes only a certain distance toward understanding Fischl's all-American usage of pet dogs. The possibility of beastiality — a more demonstrative, antisocial, and obvious perversion than voyeurism — is a perhaps not unimportant side issue in Fischl's pictures: another example of "perversion by implication." The real point is sociological: the role of pets in the modern anomic world, which Fischl conveys so beautifully through his Hollywoodesque effects (and a version of Warholesque neutrality), as the most satisfactory objects of love. *They* don't toy with one's affections, nor resist one's advances. They are the perfect infantile fetishes, absolutely satisfying narcissistically, love objects which don't shield themselves from one's voyeuristic looking and don't expect more from one, as the big naked women seem to. Animals come to us in all their nakedness, psychological as well as physical — which is why, sometimes, Fischl seems to equate, at least for the moment of leisure when they are simply there, with no expectations (thus enhancing their immediacy), his women with animals, dumb pets. Indeed, in *Dog Days,* the animal/human, pet/person equation — the pet perhaps as symbolic of the essence of the modern person at his or her natural best — is universal and direct. Fischl suggests that the identification with or fetishizing of a pet is perhaps the most archaic form of identification possible, and thus the one most restorative of one's natural, healthy narcissism.

If, as Kohut writes, "the object of the creative interest is invested with narcissistic libido" — "the narcissistic nature of the creative act" is its inmost nature[4] — then one can say that Fischl offers us the most sophisticated yet upfront narcissism one has seen for a long time in art. He articulates both the "early childhood fear of being alone, abandoned, unsupported" that is so crucial a part of narcissistic experience (recurring with special anguish in adolescence), [5] and the elementary voyeuristic strategies by which the child in one gives itself supporting company, whether animal or human. Fischl himself has said, in a statement for his February 1982 exhibition at the Edward Thorp Gallery, that "central" to his work is

> *the feeling of awkwardness and self-consciousness that one experiences in the face of profound emotional events in one's life. These experiences, such as death, or loss, or sexuality, cannot be supported by a life style that has sought so arduously to deny their meaningfulness, and a culture whose fabric is so worn out that its public rituals and attendant symbols do not make for adequate clothing . . . . Each new event is a crisis, and each crisis . . . fills us with much the same anxiety that we feel when, in a dream, we discover ourselves naked in public.*[6]

Neither modern high culture nor modern middle-class life style offers support in one's narcissistic suffering. Rarely do either even acknowledge, in a serious way, the self's feeling of inadequacy and abandonment, its narcissistic anxiety and loneliness. (Bohemian culture offers a narcissistic satisfaction of sorts through the "alternate" extended family experience — the postfamily familialism of the outsider in-group — it claims to offer.) Fischl's pictures are about the failure even of bohemian, punk, or whatever culture to offer an adequate support system for the individual suffering from a narcissistic feeling of helplessness, worthlessness, or sheer uncertainty of self. Thus a mood of contained despondency is pervasive in Fischl. His quasi-Hemingwayesque abruptness is one artistic way of bringing his painful subject matter under control. It is hard to tell whether its use is ironical. In general, Fischl's adolescent is an allegorical personification of the tragically narcissistic infant in all of us — the universal regressive narcissistic component in the self.

The brilliance of Fischl's mimesis of the modern world is perhaps at its clearest in his subtle use of the slickness — a form of callousness — it uses to mask narcissistic injury to make it manifest. The slick style of the popular view of everyday life embeds us all the more in self-loss and mutes a terrifying self-consciousness. Fischl's use of populist realism — populist voyeuristic style — to communicate unpopular recognition of modern existence has a bitter edge to it. His soap operatic voyeuristic style does not neutralize its human subject, in the expected way, but, on the contrary, undermines the masterful modern subject by making its infantile basis painfully clear. Its own slick style of mastery is turned against it. This is an artistic triumph, considering the built-in power of media style to neutralize experience into painless information. Fischl shows that despite itself media style can be revelatory of what is profoundly immanent in the human psyche; media style can be put to humanistic use. Television can become candid to the point of brutal psychological realism. Fischl's television-type coverage of modern subjectivity reveals more of reality than meets the eye.

NOTES

1.. Heinz Kohut, *The Analysis of the Self* (New York: International Universities Press, 1971), 99.

2. John E. Gedo, *Beyond Interpretation; Toward a Revised Theory for Psychoanalysis* (New York: International Universities Press, 1979), 115.

3. Jay R. Greenberg and Stephen A. Mitchell, *Object Relations in Psychoanalytic Theory* (Cambridge: Harvard University Press, 1983), 124-26.

4. Kohut, 315.

5. Kohut, 319.

6. Eric Fischl, in a press release issued by the Edward Thorp Gallery, New York, February 1982.

Corrupting Realism: Four Probes Into a Body of Work

Bruce W. Ferguson

DANGER: Curatorial WARNING

Catalogue texts and photographic reproductions may seriously overdetermine the meanings of works of art by emphasis, omission, or other privileges of authority.

I. A History of Props and Figures

Eric Fischl's first public explorations away from his formal education in high modernist abstraction took the form of a cautious declaration.[1] In the catalogue issued in conjunction with his one-person exhibition in the fall of 1975, he reprinted quotations, phrases, connotative words and short narratives, complete with spelling and/or typing errors, to accompany the paintings/objects reproduced in photographs. Texts and images performed an uneasy liaison, directed but disruptive. *Bridge Shield Shelter,* the subtitle of the publication, indexed some possible, even contradictory, associations to the work. The three-word caption also functioned as an analogy for some of the opposing impulses to make art: as a structure for movement or transfer, as symbolic defense or surrogate self, and as a place of suspension or possible contemplation.

In introducing literary but not literal aspects to his work at the level of visibility, Fischl was consciously engaged in making work which sought an audience formerly excluded by modernist tautology. This practice was common to many of his generation, often in the previously neglected and marginalized productions of video, sound works, installations and performances. Speaking of this concept of an audience Fischl has said: "Art is like theater. In theater, if you want to whisper, you have to whisper loudly enough so that the audience hears you, and the audience also has to know it's a whisper."[2] These transgressions to theatricality, primarily through figuration, narrative devices and viewer contingencies, were informed by the crucial atmosphere of theory and practice from extra-art academic researches. Artists took recourse in linguistics, psychoanalytic writings, anthropology, media and communications studies or other models, and particularly in feminist discourse on various contents which had repositioned the subjective, or subject, as a social and political condition. The autonomy of the visual was infiltrated by the verbal. The admission was that the nonverbal is never isolated from the verbal and is understood in affiliation with it. These artists could aspire to vital agency and relevance by rejection of the self-reflexive rigidity of high modernism — a technical mode without humor or irony, and hence, without contradiction.

Adam and Eve, as everyone knows
lived in the Garden, without any clothes. . .

Eric Fischl[3]

Fischl intensified this exploration over the next three years in rhymes, songs, drawings, one mural, and a collaboration with two other artists which resulted in a performance.[4] Texts and images acted as 'props' for one another. 'Props' is used here simply to refer to incomplete support systems. They situated each other in a minimally secured semantic environment, two signifiers vying, reinforcing and collapsing simultaneously — familiar and strange, *"contaminated" — Derrida.* The larger overlapping glassine drawings, without texts, similarly functioned as props for an ongoing story. Their easy movability and transparency (Figs. 6 and 7) denied a completed stable image, requiring meanings elicited by a narrative response.

One of the designated props in the performance, *Excerpts from the Prayers for Our Sisters,* was an image, previously drawn with penlight by Fischl, on exposed photographic paper. He painted developer on the image during the performance until it appeared before the audience. At the conclusion, the safelight was turned off and the unfixed image folded back to darkness, emphasizing the *process* per se and the image's partial status within that narrative. The props in all the drawings were simple — drawn or lettered in a discursive style. Beds, sleds, houses or tables and chairs, with single words or phrases on occasion, were the support system for a series of narrative incidents, units of drama. A table was turned upside down, for instance, to suggest a domestic or psychological boundary or a vehicle. The props stressed transformation, potential motion, instability, changea bility, conversion, performance and agency.

Excluding props, other prominent motifs can be identified within the same corpus of work. One of those is the interfamilial relationships shown through figuration. The nuclear family is an institutionalized unit in society which contains ethical, erotic and social implications. In Fischl's work, family arrangements have ranged from the uncomfortably stable to the actively transgressive. From 1975 to 1979, the members or characters in the drawings *(tableaux-vivants,* in effect) were portrayed as archetypal, transnational and mythopoetic figures. The adult male stood for Father-Adam-Fisherman and the adult female stood for Mother-Eve-Housewife. Initially, the protagonists were represented in texts by their absent voices. They were figures of speech, so to speak. The props — houses or fish, for example — were proposed as analogies for the domestic dialogue. The captions reproduced a form of votive, claiming the power of prayer or litany. A related text reads:

Her prayers were always simple:
Sea be calm like this bath
Sea be fruitful like a woman[5]

As images, people were highly general-

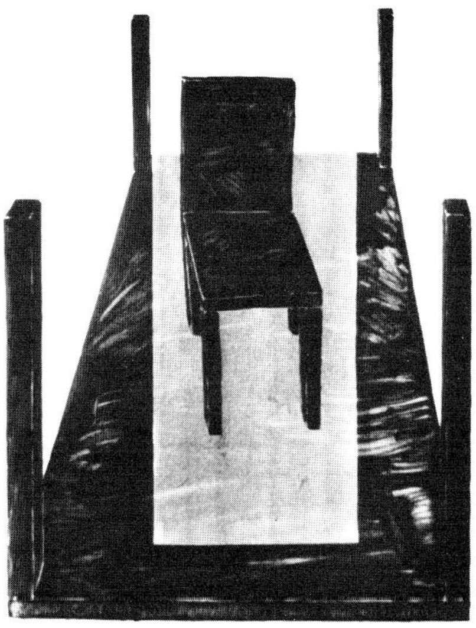

Fig. 6. *Untitled* 1979 - glassine drawing

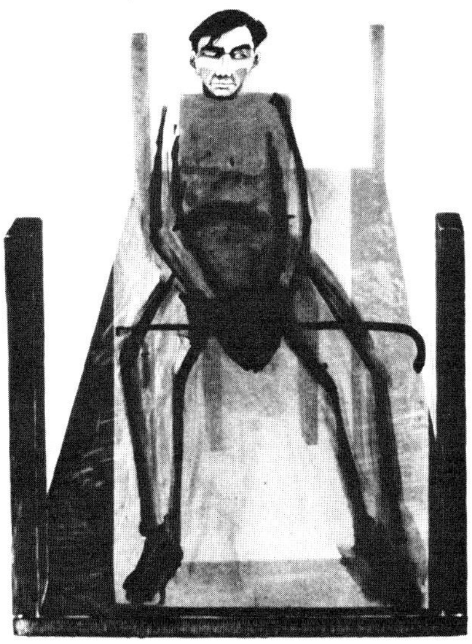

Fig. 7. *Untitled* 1979 - glassine drawing

ized types, sometimes just black silhouettes, related to a notion of cross-cultural human cycles. In some larger glassines, heads were elaborated, given illusionistic rendering for psychological import. The bodies tended to be outlines, two-dimensional props for the head.

REACH EACH OTHER (Fig. 8), a triptych drawing, exemplifies a more naturalistic stage in terms of style of this re-enactment of a familial sentiment, a style which is hesitant in its ambition and intent. The woman is contained in water in two of the images, performing a patient and silent ritual of movement, sympathetic magic to protect the man who is vulnerable in an empty container on the water. The cry in this particular text, for it is surely no command, is to bridge the space, the time, the sexes — to touch the OTHER. It is not clear whether the cry issues from the woman, the man or an unseen narrator in the work. The tentativeness of this cry, the tragic/comic nature of difference itself, is reinforced by the equally unsure ink lines.

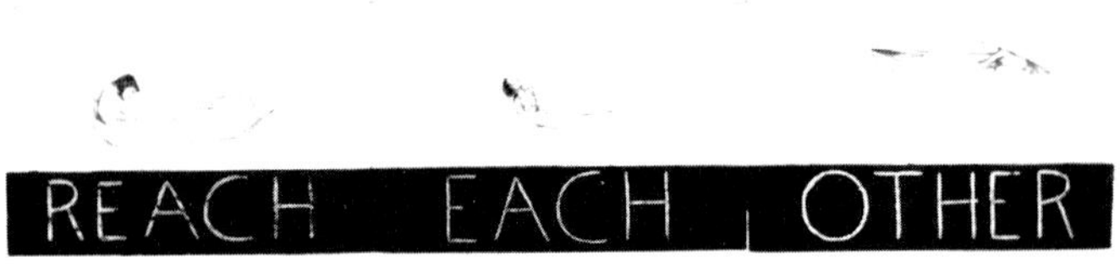

Fig. 8. *REACH EACH OTHER* - Collection of the National Gallery of Canada, Ottawa.

These images are again analogies for the process of art making. They are as much pleas for communication as they are admissions of its very difficulty. They are provisional attempts to engage a viewer/reader at a point of active mutuality. The doubt and anxiety of any artist seeking an audience, reconciliation with or recognition of the OTHER is the hidden motif of these works.

II. A History of Locations and Roles

For Fischl, and other artists then and now, reconsideration of representational elements offers the same promise of embattlement that abstraction had provided for earlier generations. The engagé, neo-realist or antimodernist climate of the 1970s was not *retardataire* or a conspiracy of the bourgeois marketplace as has been fearfully suggested, but instead was the conscious and intuitive shift from the metaphoric to the metonymic, from the private to the social, that seems to mark irregularly the condition we know as modern.[6] Fischl, for instance, considered seriously the (then) underrated works of the blatantly imagistic Philip Guston, Malcolm Morley, Paterson Ewen or Richard Artschwager, as well as the psychodynamic narrative performances of Laurie Anderson or Vito Acconci. Simultaneously, he responded in an integral way to the music and lyrics of a popular cult figure such as Patti Smith or to the vignettes quintessential to a Robert Altman film. His reading of a book such as Joseph Heller's *Something Happened,* the story of an American father's tragedy, with its discussions of potential incest or family malfunction, might find resonance directly in an image (Fig 9). In speaking of this move to the figurative, Fischl has said: "So then I began trying to get things that at least everyone could see, so they wouldn't say, 'I like the weight of this or that, or the way one color pushes off another.' Instead they would say, 'Why is that person doing that to that person?' or 'What's happening here?' "[7] Fischl could also take into account his immediate environment at that time — Nova Scotia. Although the works were ahistorical, they had a particular significance in that community, as the representations were of both local and larger issues, surface and deep structure.[8]

The examples outlined are indications of the collapse of distinctions between high and popular art, the acknowledgement of which has been endemic in so-called postmodernism. They are not meant as a hierarchical genealogy of direct influences. These and other items had a separate weight of importance. But they do point to Fischl's increasing preoccupation with placing meaning and content over formal invention. There is no seminal moment when such a decision was made; rather there was a series of gradual increments which could be measured by his growing ability in traditional drawing skills as well as by a clarification of themes. Over a period of a year and a half, Fischl had explored the problematics of performance and had completed one work, *Excerpts from the Prayers for Our Sisters.* The exigencies of this art form, i.e. the technology needed, the dependence upon others, the conditions imposed by each particular architecture, the need for multiple skills to effect a text and the ephemerality, all encouraged Fischl to reconsider painting, which he had abandoned with his rejection of abstraction. For Fischl, the return was also related to painting's ability to provide a moment, not a lifting from the flow of information, but a conscious building of a poignant and urgent reality. Into 1979, his work hovered between the poles of romance and realism, between the modes of metaphor and metonymy, or combinations of both, but his momentum was towards a fully contextualized representation within a convincing fictive space — that of painting. The works aspired to a contemporary social context, to conditions of history which underlie all realist activity.

In depicting referents, Fischl undertook a concentrated program of realism, the attitude of observation in which the details of context could provide credibility. Things have a psychological value as well as a social one. Chosen arbitrarily from a series of homogeneous products, they become invested with personal history, projected values. Possession and memory are delivered to an object. Objects are history. Objects also stage space, delineate experience and affect behavior.

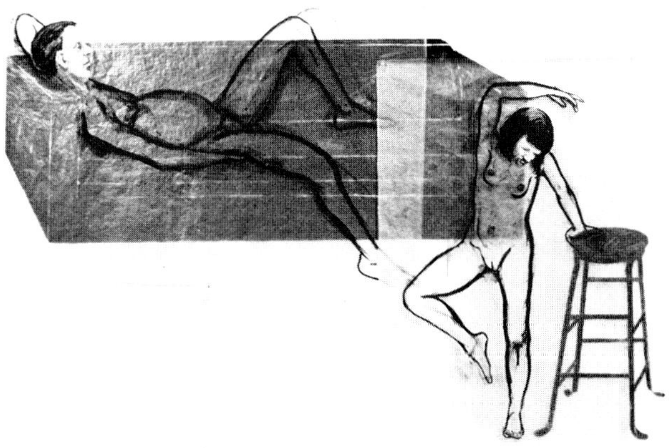

Fig. 9. *Family Scene*

The props in the drawings became specific things, certain things. Objects like fans, a Coleman cooler, a particular stool, a brand of television set (Fig. 10), a tricycle were manifested in graphics that also were becoming more conventionalized illusions. The things — the wading pool and the plastic and chrome chairs in *Sleepwalker* (Cat. 1) — are constrained pictorially by the need to represent functionally a world already known, catalogued through experience and images. But it is this very familiarity of the locations which opens the possibility of belief in the fictive subject. In its convention of resemblance to the world, a painting is understood as a fiction, as an already interpreted world.

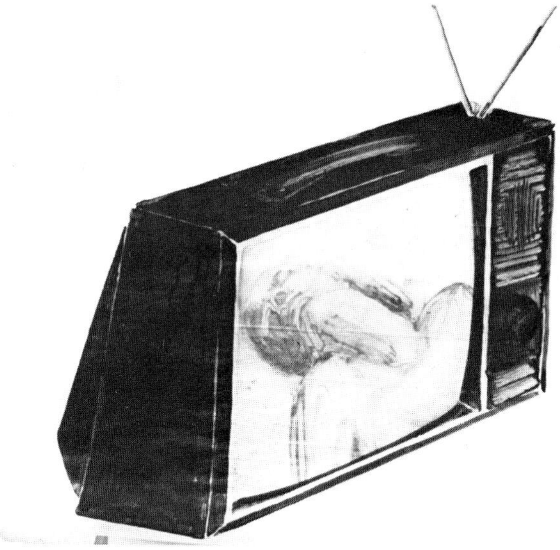

Fig. 10. *Television* 1978

And it is only in fiction, where nothing is left out, where relations can be revealed under close inspection, that we can experience the finite. *It is her velvet neck ribbon, her bracelets and her earrings, her flowers, her cat and her dangling pump heel that made Manet's courtesan a believable image of sexuality.*

The painted people began to play roles, to be assigned contemporary Western lifestyles. The themes — internal and external fears threatening domesticity, numb isolation in the face of intimacy, conjugal rift and reconciliation, death and separation and ubiquitous sexuality — were established in the social locations of daily life.[9] Rather than stiffly iconic, people were painted from the vocabulary of a well-known body language, *Barthes's "classification of stereotypes."* They were poses from an omnipresent lexicon; that is, they became recognizable, foregrounded by a popular consciousness of a shared culture. To this end, Fischl has increasingly relied on photographs, a quotable source, from advertisements, snapshots, porno pix, book and magazine illustrations, etc., with gestural and cultural characteristics. The hand of the boy scratching the thigh as his other hand adjusts the TV in *Slumber Party* (Fig. 5), the self-protective hug and awkwardly overlapping foot of the girl in *New House* (Cat. 13), the bowed head and groin clutch of the pyjamaed boy in *Time for Bed* (Fig. 4). . . . Aren't these images we've seen before? Aren't these gestures part of our culture's repertoire? *Don't Olympia's left hand and her crossed legs with a definite knee repeat the code of 19th century stereoscopic coquetry of provocation and pretense, giving her a role which is not that of the idealized nude?*

Like the observation of objects, this is the realist figure of synecdoche being applied — the substitution of the part for the whole, or the reverse — standing for a set of role categories: age, gender, class, status, lifestyle. The relentless mundanity of surface descriptions, the credible evidence of the objects and gestures in detail, provoke the emergence of underlying social, sexual and psychological drama, as, for instance, in one painting entitled *The Day the Shah Ran By (not illustrated).* This fictional use of historical characters produces a minor or modest effect, according to Barthes in speaking of realist fiction. He says: "It is precisely this minor importance which gives the historical character its *exact* weight of reality: this *minor* is the measure of authenticity: Diderot, Mme de Pompadour, later Sophie Arnould, Rousseau, d'Holbach are introduced into the fiction laterally, obliquely, *in passing*, painted on the scenery, not represented on the stage; for if the historical character were to assume its *real* importance, the discourse would be forced to yield it a role which would, paradoxically, make it less real. . . ."[10] The procedure of synecdoche generates the believable fiction. Actual commodities specify locations, and mediated gestures or body codes specify the roles of individuated social beings.

Fischl has subsumed the catalogue of signifiers into the gestural and sensuous surface of painting: paint acting as image, paint performing the fiction of representation. This deviates from the more predominant direct use of photographic materiality that marks much of 'appropriated' contemporary artworks. Photography has an inherent tendency towards enclosure (taken photos, not made photos) which produces irony, simple cynicism or rote ruptures in its use as 'appropriated'. Donald Kuspit has argued that "Photography can function this way because it represents the domination of social authority through its 'spying' on our existence. Photographic documentation, seemingly all-pervasive, has come to represent an authoritarian penetration of existence," and later, "Photography, with its heterogeneity, mechanical procedures, and seriality, symbolizes the powerful control a technologically advanced society has on existence."[11] And yet, in the late part of the twentieth century, all painting (all art) participates in this popular cultural inheritance, *"the Image-World" — Sontag,* the overproduction of image-signs, and is foregrounded to produce what Kuspit has called a "kind of artificial natural expression" of paint on canvas.

This is not to say that Fischl's work cannot be seen within an art history puzzle of referents. The boy's shadow in *Sleepwalker* or the girl's shadow in *New House* strongly recalls the shadow in Edvard Munch's *Puberty*, or one of the women in *Sisters* (Cat. 20) is a reinterpretation of one of Paul Outerbridge's photographed 'nudes'. *After the Kill* might seem an ecologically motivated update of Courbet's *The Wave*, and Fischl's empty lounge chairs, witholding, withdrawing or silencing, provide a similar erotic charge to earlier Hockney uses. Or Tom Wesselman's *Great American Nude,* with its active TV set, might be seen as a prototype of Fischl's many uses of TV as a part of the still life.

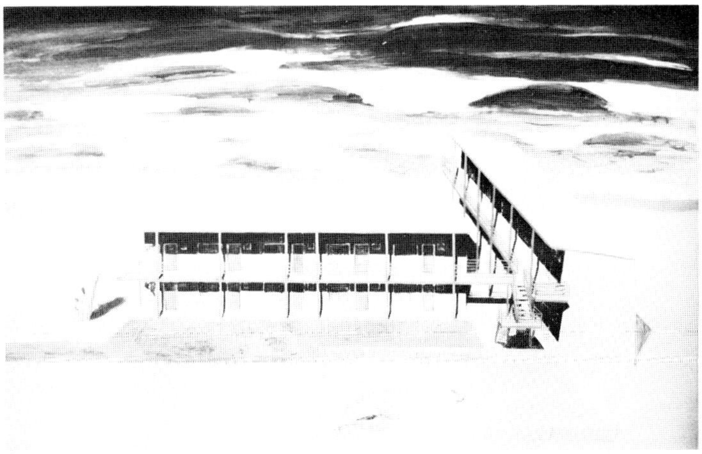

Fig. 11. *Last Resort* 1979

Although Fischl does not actually utilize the distancing devices of photography materially (using them as *aide-mémoire* for transformation), his works would seem to take advantage of one of its most popular forms — cinema. His use of cinematic references or devices has been hinted at by many writers reading his images.[12] In my description of the motion from props to locations, and from figures to roles, there is, in effect, a deliberate progression from the proto-cinematic devices in 19th century realists like Dégas and Hardy to the full and necessary cinematic consciousness today of artists and audiences alike.[13] As artists, Goldstein, Longo, Salle and Sherman could be cited, among others. This memory of film, perhaps more so than either painting or photographic

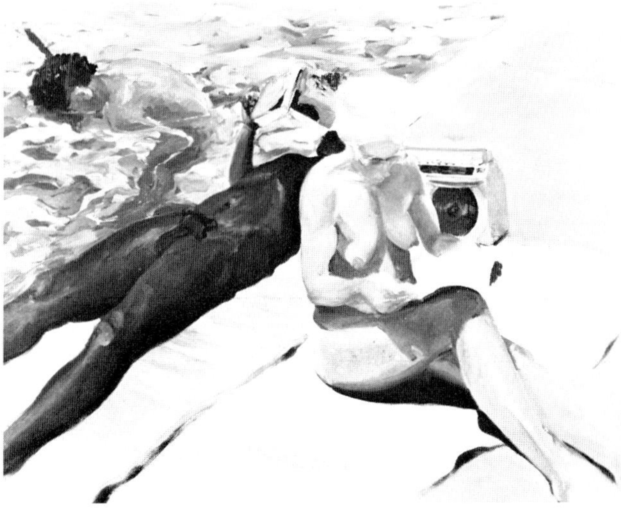

Fig. 12. *Untitled* 1984

references, is one of the aspects of the popular consciousness that allows easy access to these paintings.

The establishing shot, as it were, is *Last Resort* (Fig. 11), an aerial or crane long shot of a motel with its suggestions of a restless, mobile society and clandestine encounters. It is *Psycho, Welcome to L.A.* or *Tender Mercies* as much as Walker Percy's *Love in the Ruins* or any of Edward Hopper's motel/hotel environments that inform this image. The ocean and beach are at once nature and culture, where leisure and tans are worked at in a mockery of free time. The primitive sculpture, with its island significance, whether authentic or a prop, manifests itself as a *difference* from the juxtaposed culture of Americana. And the enclosed pool suggests an immersion which is sanitized and denatured. This is a prologue of images and formal devices (water is a fluid atmosphere of many works, natural or cultural, used to distort, move or alienate) which will be encountered later. This is one of the environments in which Fischl's cast of characters often play out their narrative moments. The image in the title's punning establishing shot suggests movement, transience and instability. In short, a moving picture.

The backyard suburbs, the beaches, the motel or guest rooms with open suitcases all suggest locations for the stories, time-sharing plans to use the real estate idiom of condominium resorts. They are impermanent environments for a dislocated behavior. Coexistence without connection. The suburbs could be anywhere in North America and the beaches are far-flung vacation spots from Greece to the Côte d'Azur, to Florida, to California, to the Caribbean. They are the rootless structures contrived for commerce, locations for structured fictions. Characters are given 'tags' for empathetic identification: an amputated arm, a radio, a TV, or book, a pet or more complex psychological associative names such as klepto, reader, show-off or the one who sleeps with the TV on, just as film characters are. There are no stars, however; characters are anonymous, *"typages" to use Eisenstein's key term for amateur actors.*

The diptychs resemble the use of a wipe or split-screen as seen in *Dog Days* (Cat. 18). A parallel activity, either a flashback or a flash-forward effect, is summoned, an elision which produces a curious equivalence through a filmic juxtaposition. Some paintings are grisaille, black to white tones, suggestive of the serious expressive associations with a *noir* film drama as in *Grief* (Cat. 9). And the gestural body language of silent film (or *Rear Window* which is an implicit retrospective of possible liaisons in silent film) informs the bodies as much as references to paintings or photographs do. It is even possible, particularly by positioning paintings side by side, to see certain figurative images frame by frame, reappearing as though in sequence. The boy, woman and man in *Saviour Mother, Save Your Love(r)* (Cat. 19) could easily be the same characters in *Untitled* 1984 (Fig. 12), a compilation whose order would determine the direction of the narrative. This allusion to film history or a shared cinematic consciousness does not fix specific films or scenes in some sort of translation, nor would a glossary of film techniques find a term-for-term literality. It merely points to the admission of that existence as a tool for accessibility.

The complex of painting, photographic, literary and filmic references which interweave and are embedded in these paintings accent the fictional, the constructed nature of the images. The apparentness of the *mise en scène*, the genre of realism's key method, is the conception to stage the fictional narrative. Fischl's paintings often imply a non-synch sound track of prerecorded sound with their TVs and figures lost in a reverie of sound on ear phones. *19th century realist paintings have a prevision of silent films' accompanying music if we think of Manet's Tuileries, Seurat's musicians or Degas' operas.*

III. Reading

> *The elimination of the human relationship in artistic representation causes the vacuum which makes all of us suffer in various degrees.*
>
> Max Beckmann[14]

Fischl has spoken of reading a Max Beckmann painting and it is not surprising that he would find fascination in Beckmann's *Departure* (Fig. 13) with its latent multiplicity of associations, including the gnostical-ethical connotations.[15] He had already employed the ambiguous symbol of the fish and the triptych structure with its quasi-religious authority. The implication for narrativity on the part of the viewer was also significant. Reading is a grasping at meaning, a process of active interpretation, in which tension is maintained and continued until the end, particularly in the case of a text where there is a contiguous physical and temporal sequence. A reading can result in a passive consumption, where a reader reproduces an author's meanings. Or a reading can more positively result in the active initiation of new meanings. This is similar to images but the tension is continually held, or reheld, because there is no continuation and the conclusion of the narrative is always deferred to the viewer. As is suggested here, signifiers can be

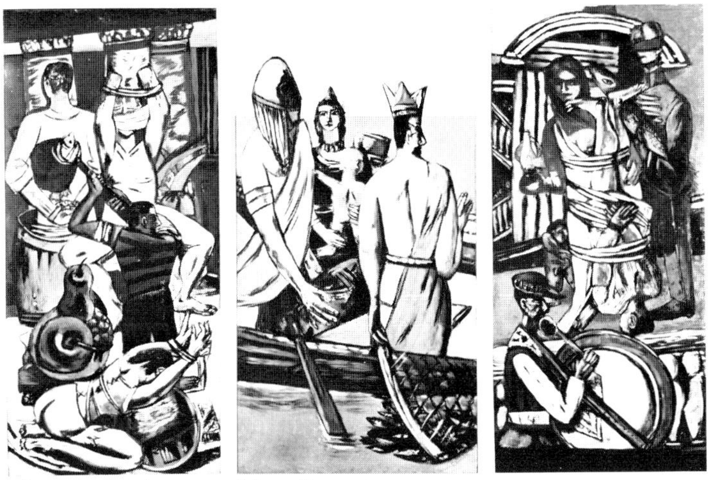

Fig. 13. Beckmann, Max *Departure* (1932 - 33) Oil on canvas; triptych, center panel 215.3 x 115.2 cm, side panels each 215.3 x 99.7 cm. Collection, The Museum of Modern Art, New York, Given anonymously.

used for either conformity or consequence. Or to index art or the world.

As I have written before in relation to these works: "Single-frame images do not conform to the necessary sequential structure of a complete narrative. But they do represent an absent event; they index another time and place, whether fictional or not. More importantly, they suggest narrativity: that is, a story to be fulfilled by a viewer. Just as in photographs, there is an image with a before, and an after (although they are not given). These works are 'occasions' for story-telling, potential narratives, descriptions of a moment in an event to be imagined by the viewer. Their full meaning lies in our identification and complicity in furnishing the larger story. This is analogous to the reading of a text, in which each reader produces a variation of the text, a facsimile dependent upon his/her receptiveness, comprehension, psychological set and social bias."[16] This aspect of narrativity set in motion by the partial or incomplete text of the narrator has been recognized and commented on by other writers with regard to Fischl's work. Kate Linker has said: "As in film stills, the disjointed images yield only fragmentary information: the narrative remains suspended, and the responsibility to forge meaning, fusing contradictions and developing inferences devolves upon the viewer."[17]

This is the process of reading an image. The viewer is always a complicit voyeur and a revisionist in the face of a realist image which encourages narrativity. These images desire interpretation and not the fixed state of authoritative truth. Fischl continues to insert the reader into paintings as a reminder of this function of text, narrativity and interpretation.

IV. Corrupt Realism

I think that the best art that's being done today in America deals with the crisis of American identity, the failure of the American dream, and how overtaxed we are, both politically and in terms of what we think things mean.

The only difference is now we don't believe it, whereas then everything seemed totally possible. But we've watched the way America has grown and acted and it doesn't match the ideal. I mean, America's not Disneyland and we can't deny it any longer. Things smell, things have edges, people can get hurt.

Eric Fischl[18]

These statements by Fischl, together with the critical response to his works, suggest both motivations and responses which are critical of predominant neoconservative culture in America.[19] And yet, the style he employs is a form of realism, a style which is now associated with the mirroring of a bourgeois society with its assumptions of playing out what it considers natural relations, *"power, knowledge and sexuality" — Foucault.* Realism further suffers from an unfashionable theoretical status due to its use of an ordinary language of images. Realism, usually, does not seem capable of criticality but rather only of reflection, a reflection which is open to absorption by the very structures it reflects upon. How can this style be used to interrogate its subject when it seems to argue conservatively for continuity and history, not radical departure? The answer is that the expected reflection is destabilized in the relations among the images in his works. The decay or contradictions unconsciously displayed by the roles are revealed. It is, then, not the style that is at issue, but the structures for openness or relevance which encourage narrativity that allow for criticality from a viewer.

It is reading, which has been admitted, that assigns the image a status or likeness to a text. Kate Linker has identified one of the elements which record "narrative networks" in Fischl's images to effect criticality through narrativity. She relates the shuttling of narrative registers to Barthes's concept of the "writerly" text with "several entrances, none of which can authoritatively be declared to be the main one," and suggests a similar practice discernible in Beckmann's paintings with their "contradictory valences and radically opposed meanings to 'jam' metonymy, breaking the flow of literal event to insinuate the spectator's participation, and doubling the account of the narrative with the cultural or historical allusions."[20] It is these gaps, these discontinuities, *"vacant spaces" — Fielding,* which serve to deny completion by a disruptive use of realism. They corrupt its usual rhetorical and classicizing effect.

A partial list of entrance devices might be desirable at this point. Linker has said: "Notable among them are the use of equivocal objects that center or divide two unrelated activities (i.e. the beach ball in the painting of the same name, 1981) or absences, as with the vacant chairs, charged with sexual innuendoes, in *Sleepwalker* 1979."[21] Normality, by which is meant the cultural project of middle-classification, is disrupted or jammed by the presence of blacks, as well. They unfetter the chain of WASP signifiers. The voodoo doll with its far-reaching shadow atop the TV in *Slumber Party* or the third-worldly appearance of the costumed man on the beach in *Cargo Cult* (not illustrated) provides another key to open the system. The inter-racial relationship in *Saviour Mother, Save Your Love(r)* disturbs expectation (realism as reflection) by inclusion of difference. Difference, here, has a mixed name. It is fear of the unknown on one hand and glorification of the subterranean on the other. Paradise is made insecure by the new catalyst.

Adolescents, particularly the naughty boys who frequently appear, are equally fissures which expose the illegitimate side of this class of Americans. Adolescents are outlaws to the myth of normality. Their sexuality is not legitimized, their music is hidden in earphones and their literature is suspect behind closed doors. They are the lie to the ideological truth. Their presence unhinges the *"rule of silence regarding the noisiest of our preoccupations" — Foucault.* The inexpressible, the taboo of sexuality except in the privilege of the parents' bedrooms, is embodied in their intrusive nakedness. The silent regulations which govern all bodies are announced. The *Pizza Eater* (Cat. 12), with her evidently Freudian triangular 'piece' and her Lowrey coke bottle with inserted straw, is innocent, unless she is *Lolita*, of the gazes of the two older men who, in turn, could be associated with the pleasure boat and the naval ship on the horizon. In *Squirt* (not illustrated), the unconscious male aggressivity towards women by a young boy with his watergun is quietly approved by an older man who watches. Experience and innocence, pornography and puerility, already-knowing and almost-knowing are cross-indexed in the imagery as depictions of difference.[22] They are ruptures inviting curiosity and discovery, the very stimulation of narrativity.

Pets, notably dogs, point to another area of disquietude. Pets are socialized OTHERS, already mediated by the requirements of their owners and laws determining behavior. But, they are still capable of providing embarrassment. They break social codes, scatological and sexual. They transgress by unexpected reversions to natural behavior. In *A Woman Possessed* (Cat. 6), some dogs are threatening and some supportive, or at least neutral. To elaborate their presence is to provide expectations of humor or embarrassment, as well as of emotional comfort. Dogs are the choreographers of the sidewalks.

Any partial list of objects or images which act as shifters for reading would have to include the television sets and their internal images which frequently occur in these works. Fischl forecast his use of TV as a cultural icon in *TV and Thee* 1981 (not illustrated), a glassine drawing where a division of experience is made explicit by the immersion of two viewers in the light of two different TVs which they are watching. In *The Visitor* (not illustrated), the TV 'visits' as well, habitualized surrogate company. And it must be a TV which sits under a still life in *Birthday Boy* (Fig. 2) which holds the conspirators' attention away from the obvious sexual implications.[23] A TV is an object of power for all that it is held in low esteem. Its presence in the works describes a split, an environment of active passivity for the characters, an index of the technology of politicized 'entertainment' which poses as the pursuit of happiness. TV denies history and determines political agendas in the name of 'news'; it turns public events into privatized consumption by merciless socialization in the name of entertainment. As quixotic collage machines, they inscribe the OTHER as a mesmerizing world mediated by distracting images and appearances, a surrogate reality of codes hidden from the measurement of experience.

A fuller discussion of some aspects of Fischl's recent work, its history and methods, would have to include the undressing of appearances (fashion), an inventory of gazes as rehearsals for intimacy or loneliness, and painterly techniques, all of which are absent from this commentary. However, it is hoped that this series of probes, with its emphasis on the place of the viewer in relation to strategies for narrativity and critical readings through rupturing devices, will stir even further interpretation. None of this is meant to suggest that the paintings are politically correct in some way. They are not forced representations of dominated races, classes or gender. Often, in fact, they depict a state of initiation, the moment when the inheritance of the paternal order is handed down (the gaze with which we are complicit in *Pizza Eater*, the look of approval in *Squirt*), the moment when the abuse of power is not interrogated and the Oedipal is put into play. But this is their power, their strength of precision. It is these interrupted moments in our culture's story, with their further implications to be sought by the viewer, which are of importance. Because the signifiers have multiple directions, the images are corrupted. Like blasphemies or puns in a text, like the joy and the naughtiness sensed in these images, the devices of reversibility aggress the image to unveil codes and allow for new possibilities of meaning. The contribution of corrupted realism is to allow a public in, for the paintings to take on their fullest existence in their relationship to a conscientious viewer.

NOTES

1. Eric Fischl, *Eric Fischl: Bridge Shield Shelter* (Halifax: Dalhousie Art Gallery, 1975), [1 - 20].
2. Carter Ratcliff, ed., "Expressionism Today: An Artists' Symposium," *Art in America* 70(December 1982): 60-62.
3. Eric Fischl, "Eric Fischl," in *Kanadische Kunstler*, ed. Jean-Christophe Ammann (Basel: Kunsthalle, 1978), [62].
4. Rober Racine, "Festival de performances du M.B.A.M.," *Parachute* 13 (Hiver 1978): 46.
5. Fischl, "Eric Fischl," [64].
6. See Donald Kuspit, "Flak from the Radicals: The American Case Against Current German Painting, "*Expressions: New Art from Germany* (Saint Louis: Saint Louis Art Museum/Munich: Verlag, 1983), [64] for a history of the reception by critics in America to "expressionist" work.
7. Kevin Robbins, "Eric Fischl: Interview by Kevin Robbins, *Upstart* (1984): 6-7, 46.
8. Peter Perrin, "Friends of the Form," *artscanada* (February/March 1978): 44-47 is the first example of this kind of consideration. Similarly, see Jeffrey Spalding, "Eric Fischl, "*Coasts, the Sea and Canadian Art* (Stratford, Ontario: the Gallery/Stratford, 1978), where the work is treated in this context and relations drawn to Marsden Hartley for example.
9. Bruce Ferguson, "In the Middle of a Story/Au Milieu d'une Histoire," *Eric Fischl: Dessins/Drawings* (Montreal, Centre Saidye Bronfman, 1983), vii.
10. Roland Barthes, *S/Z*, trans. R. Miller (New York: Hill & Wang, 1974), 101-2.
11. Kuspit, *Expressions: New Art from Germany*, 50-51.
12. For instance, John Yau sees in "bleak venetian blinds" a reminiscence of 1950s Grade B films and Fischl's use of color ". . . is as grim and sensitive as Jean-Luc Godard's use of newsreel film strategy in *Vivre sa vie* (My life to live), where Anna Karina plays a doomed revolutionary" (John Yau, "How We Live: The Paintings of Robert Birmelin, Eric Fischl, and Ed Paschke," *Artforum* 21[April 1983]: 65). Or Lisa Liebmann, who makes important notes on ownership in her review of the print *Year of the Drowned Dog*, likens one of its versions to ". . . as in Vittorio de Sica's movie *Two Women* (1960) . . . " (Lisa Liebmann, "Eric Fischl's Year of the Drowned Dog: Eight Characters in Search of an Autumn," *Artforum* 22[March 1984]: 69). Jon R. Friedman references the movie *Quest for Fire* in discussing an exhibition of Fischl's called *Scenes from a Private Beach* (Jon R. Friedman, "Eric Fischl," *Arts Magazine* 56[June 1982]: 21). Robert Pincus-Witten uses terms like ". . . classical Freudian skin-flick" and "cinematographically framed. . . " (Robert Pincus-Witten, "Entries: Snatch and Snatching," *Arts Magazine* 56[September 1981]: 89-90). And a quote from Kate Linker is included in this text which likens the works to film stills (Kate Linker, "Eric Fischl: Involuted Narratives," *Flash Art* [January 1984]: 56-58.) Although Fischl's painting references have been cited in origins as disparate as Brueghel, Matisse and Reginald Marsh, among others, it would seem clear that cinema is both a reference for him and for today's critics as these short passages indicate. And the fact that his paintings call them up seems significant as I have tried to show.
13. See David Lodge, "Thomas Hardy as a Cinematic Artist," *Working with Structuralism* (London: Routledge & Kegan Paul, Ltd., 1981), 95-105 for this prevalent idea regarding 19th century realism. Or Stanley Cavell, *The World Viewed*, enl. ed. (Cambridge: Harvard University Press, 1979), particularly pages 41-45 on Baudelaire's prevision of film.
14. Max Beckmann, *On My Painting*, ed. Curt Valentin (New York: Buchholtz Gallery, 1941), 10.
15. Ratcliff, ed., "Expressionism Today," 60-61.
16. Ferguson, *Eric Fischl: Dessins/Drawings*, iv.
17. Kate Linker, "Eric Fischl: Involuted Narratives," *Flash Art* (January 1984): 56-58.

18. Robbins, "Eric Fischl." 58.

19. For instance, Peter Schjeldahl says: "The catastrophic failure of modern society to provide secure structures for human development has long been decried by psychologists and sociologists. A good Fischl painting is worth a mountain of studies that lend themselves so readily to intellectual and moral evasions" (Peter Schjeldahl, "Bad Boy of Brilliance," *Vanity Fair* [May, 1984]: 67-72).
Or John Bentley Mays has written: "Where art and religion once sustained values that challenged and slashed across bourgeois culture, in Fischl's vision both forces have been castrated and turned into dull objects of mass consumerism" (John Bentley Mays, "Eric Fischl Rages at the Giants of Art," *Toronto Globe and Mail*, 14 February 1981.

20. Linker, "Eric Fischl," 58.

21. Linker, "Eric Fischl," 58.

22. Adolescence is the subject and state of much American culture, as Leslie Fiedler has pointed out, for instance. Stanley Cavell offers this generalization: "In this condition, self-consciousness, for the foreseeable future, will start, and mostly continue, as embarrassment . . . . It it makes sense to speak of the Greeks as having discovered the self, or of the eighteenth and nineteenth centuries as having discovered childhood, then we can say that our recent accomplishment has been the discovery of adolescence, the point at which one's life is to be chosen and one gives one-self a name, and that our task is to discover the existence of community." (Cavell, *The World Viewed, 93-94).*

23. In a cogent text on two Fischl paintings Mario Diacono has written of this scene in *Birthday Boy:* ". . . (What divine vision outside the painting is drawing their eyes away from the Scene?)" Mario Diacono, *Eric Fischl,* (New York: Mary Boone/Michael Werner Gallery, 1984): [9].
I'm suggesting that it's a TV. Diacono makes the relationship between the "transparent metaphor" of sexuality of the still life and the bed scene and further points out the painting's relationship to Manet's *Le Déjeuner sur l'Herbe* by its exact measurement and Courbet's *Origine du Monde.* In relation to the viewer, he says: "If for Manet, 'modernity' is the pretext that sets the Painting in motion, Fischl, whose pictorial 'form' seems miraculously to bring the Subject back up to date, uses the manetian code in order to put contemporaneity into Vision — for him painting is an apparatus for summoning the viewer to Judgement and training him to Judge, or making him the Secret Subject of the painting. . . ." (Diacono, *Eric Fischl,* [9].

Catalogue of the Exhibition

All measurements are in centimeters,
height precedes width. All works are oil on canvas.

1. *Sleepwalker*
1979
183 x 274
The Downe Collection
New York, New York, U.S.A.

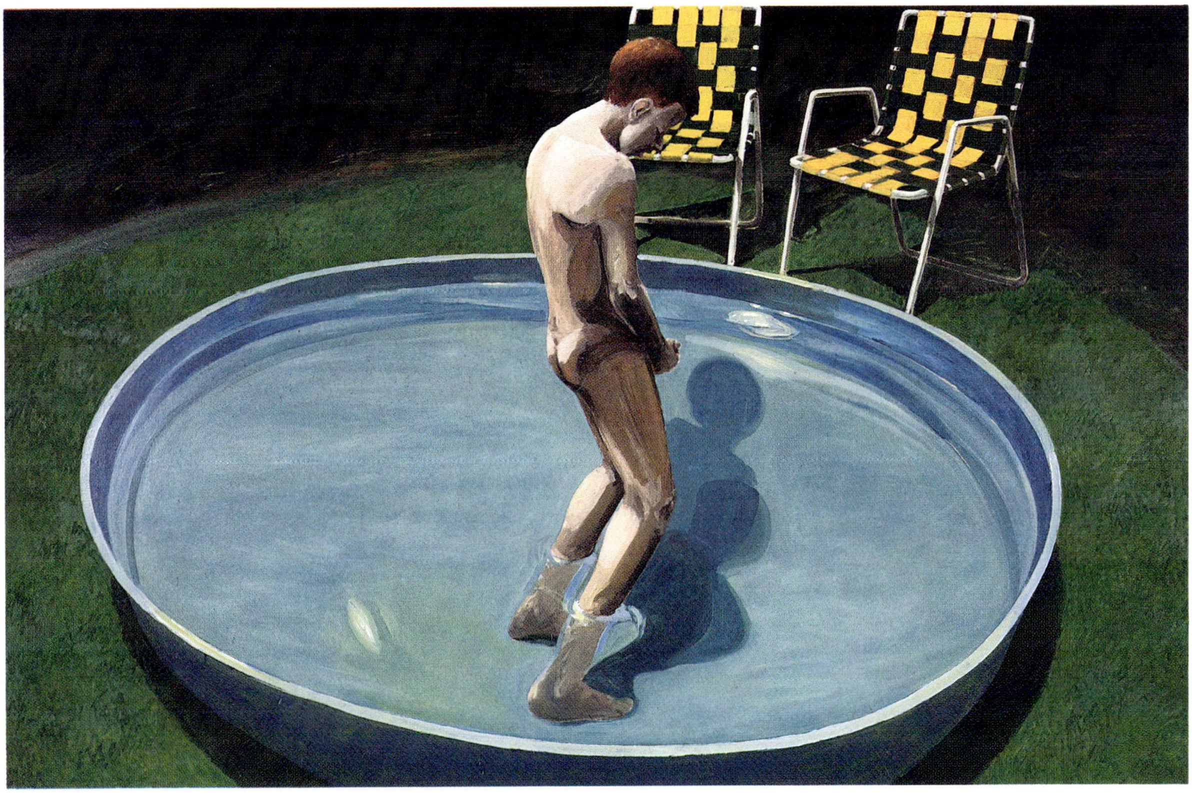

2. *A Funeral*
1980
140 x 262
Collection of Mr. Martin Sklar
New York, New York, U.S.A.

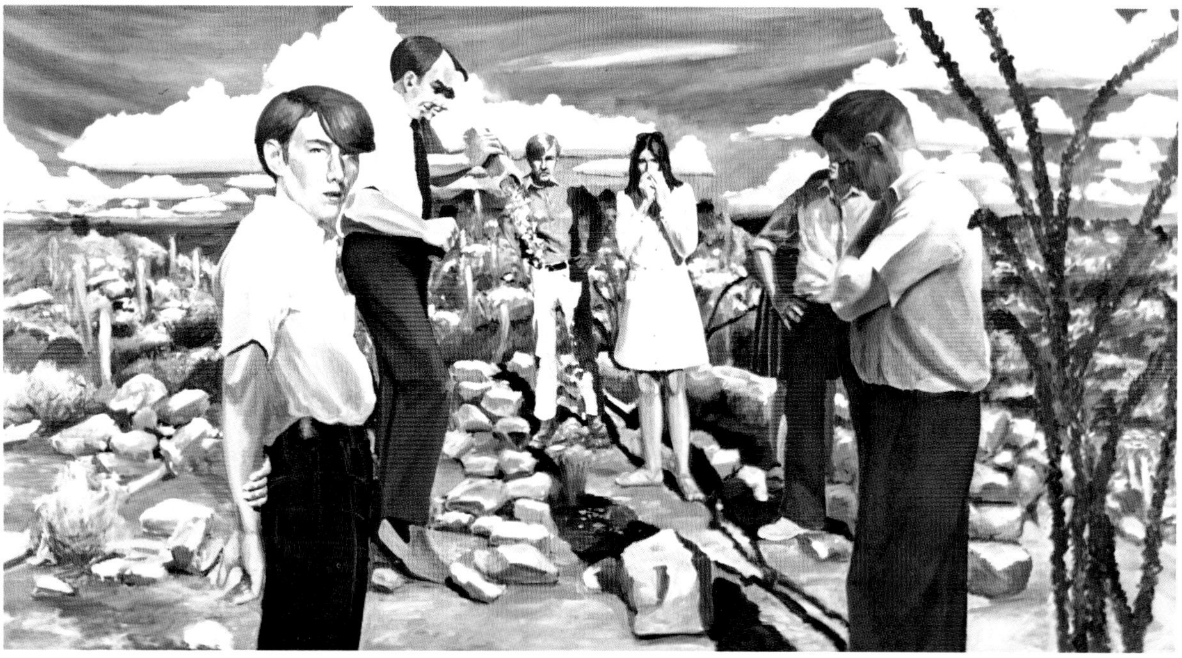

3. *Christian Retreat*
1980
183 x 244
Collection of Alcan Smelters and Chemicals Ltd.
Montreal, Quebec, Canada

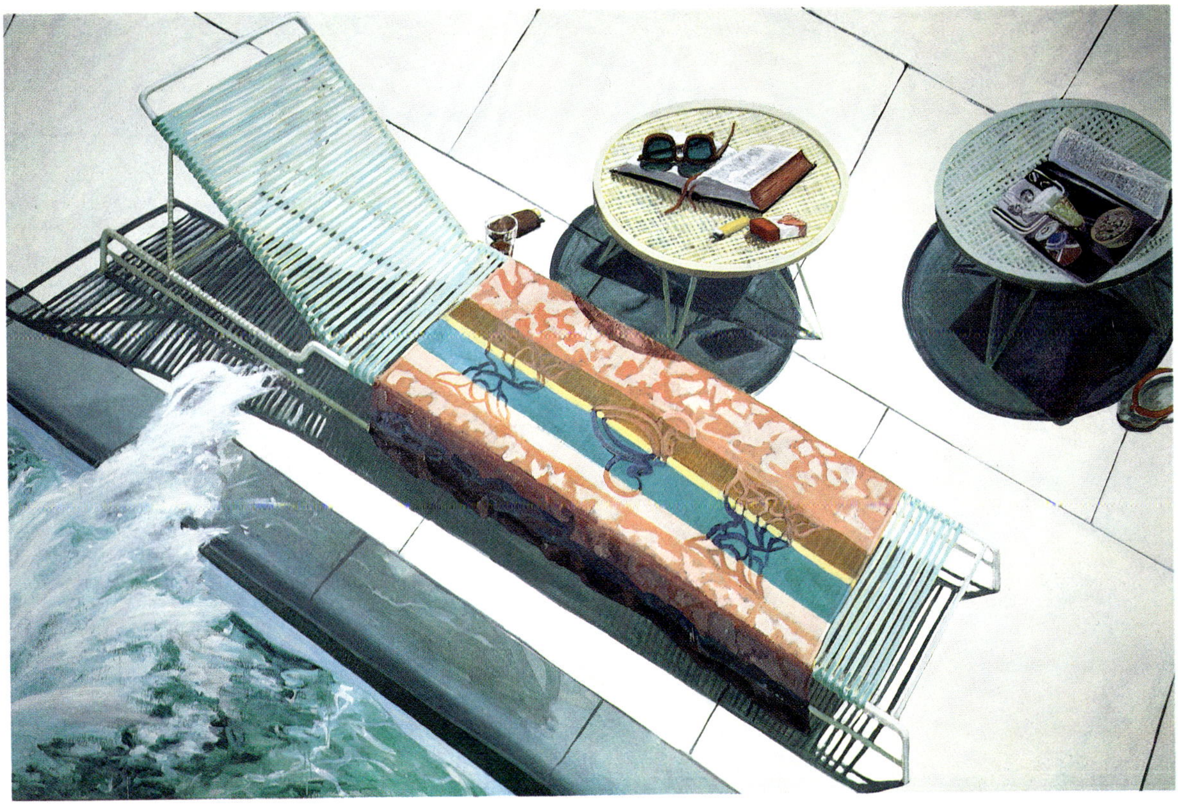

4. *Woman Surrounded by Dogs*
1980
165 x 244
Collection of Dr. and Mrs. Cecil Gilbert
Toronto, Ontario, Canada

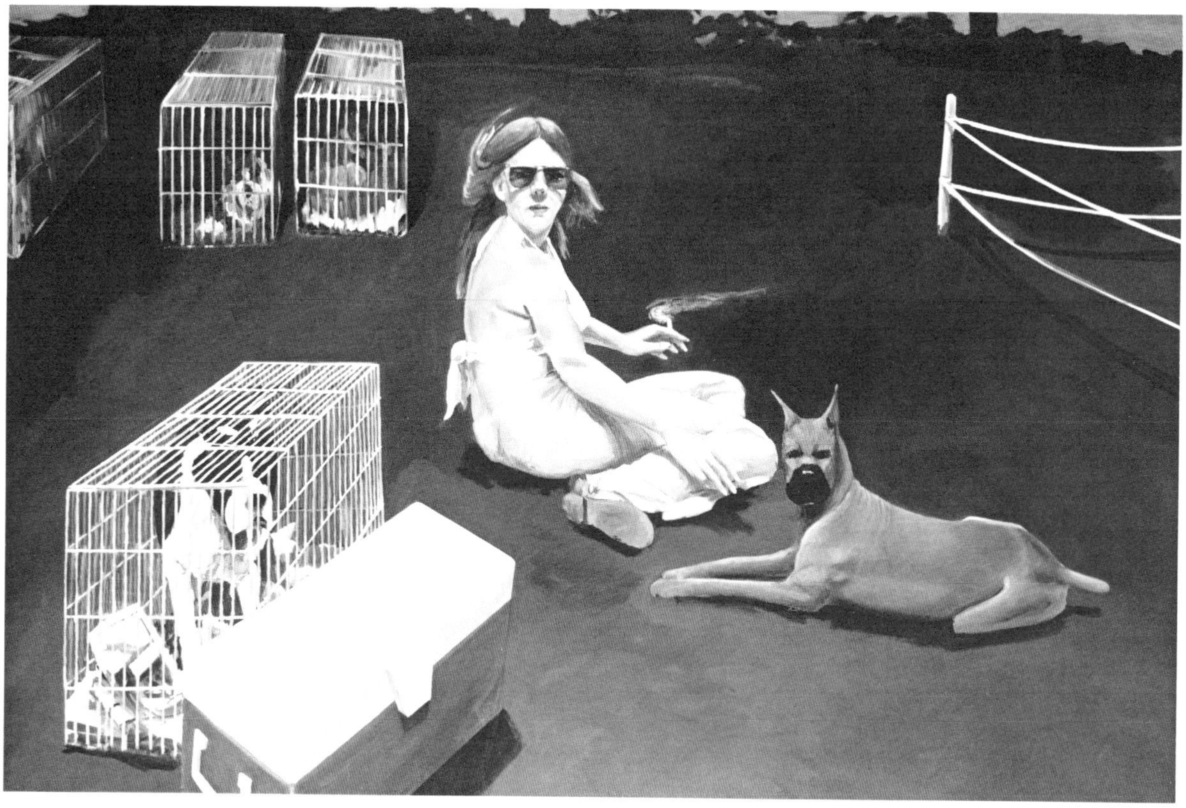

5. *Father and Son Sleeping*
1980
183 x 183
Private Collection

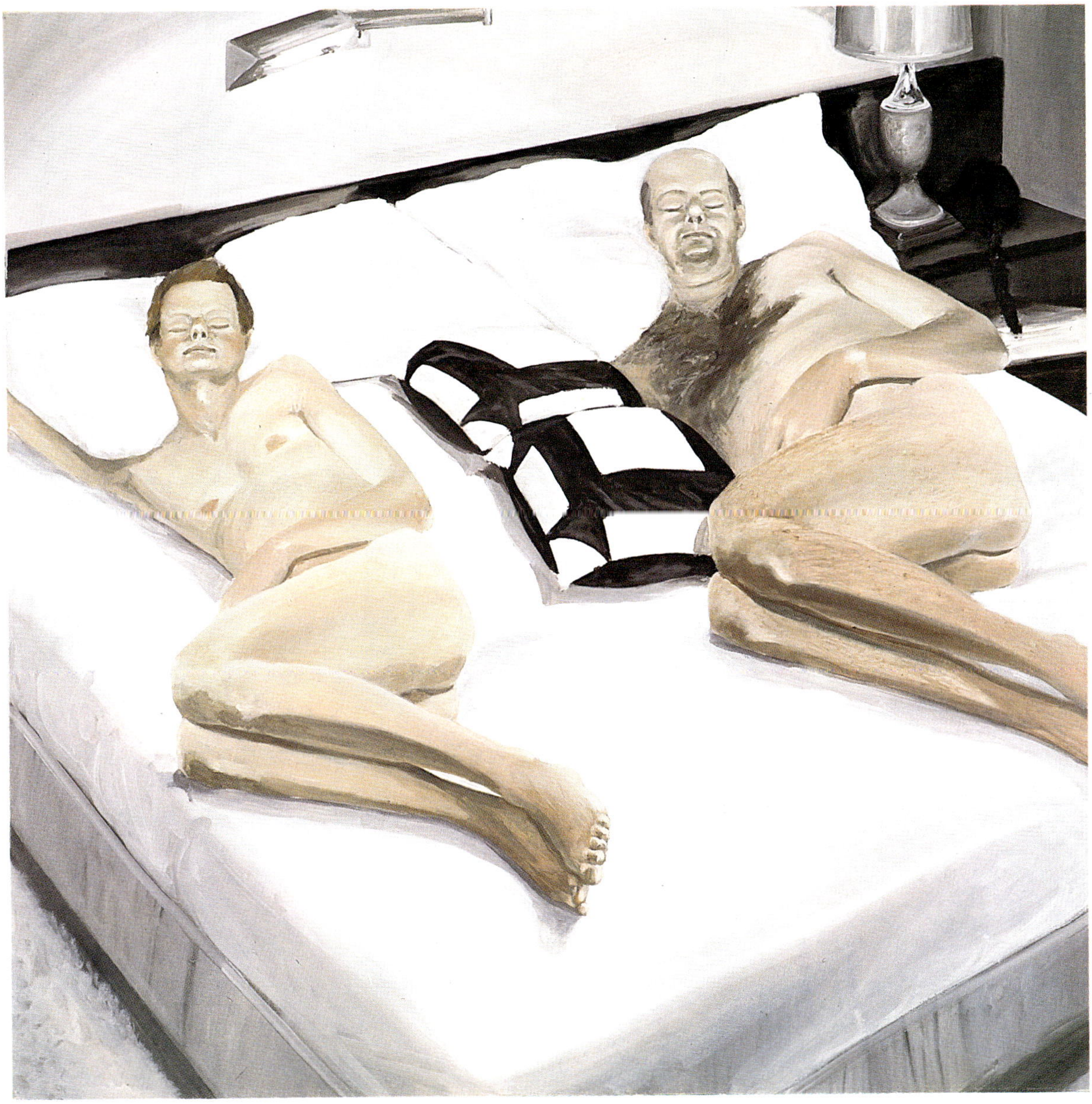

6. *A Woman Possessed*
1981
173 x 244
Collection of Sable-Castelli Gallery Ltd.
Toronto, Ontario, Canada

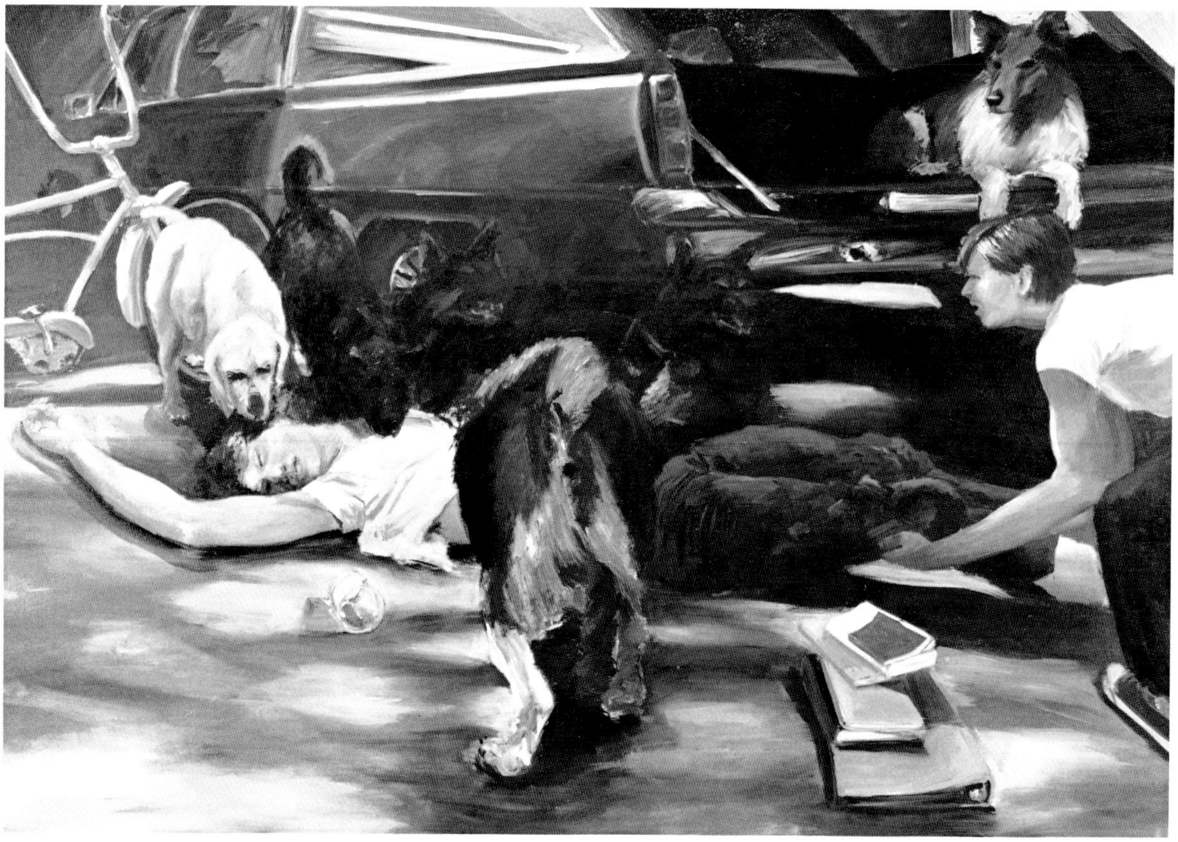

7. *The Visit II*
1981
172 x 198
Collection of Mr. Peter N. Greenwald
New York, New York, U.S.A.

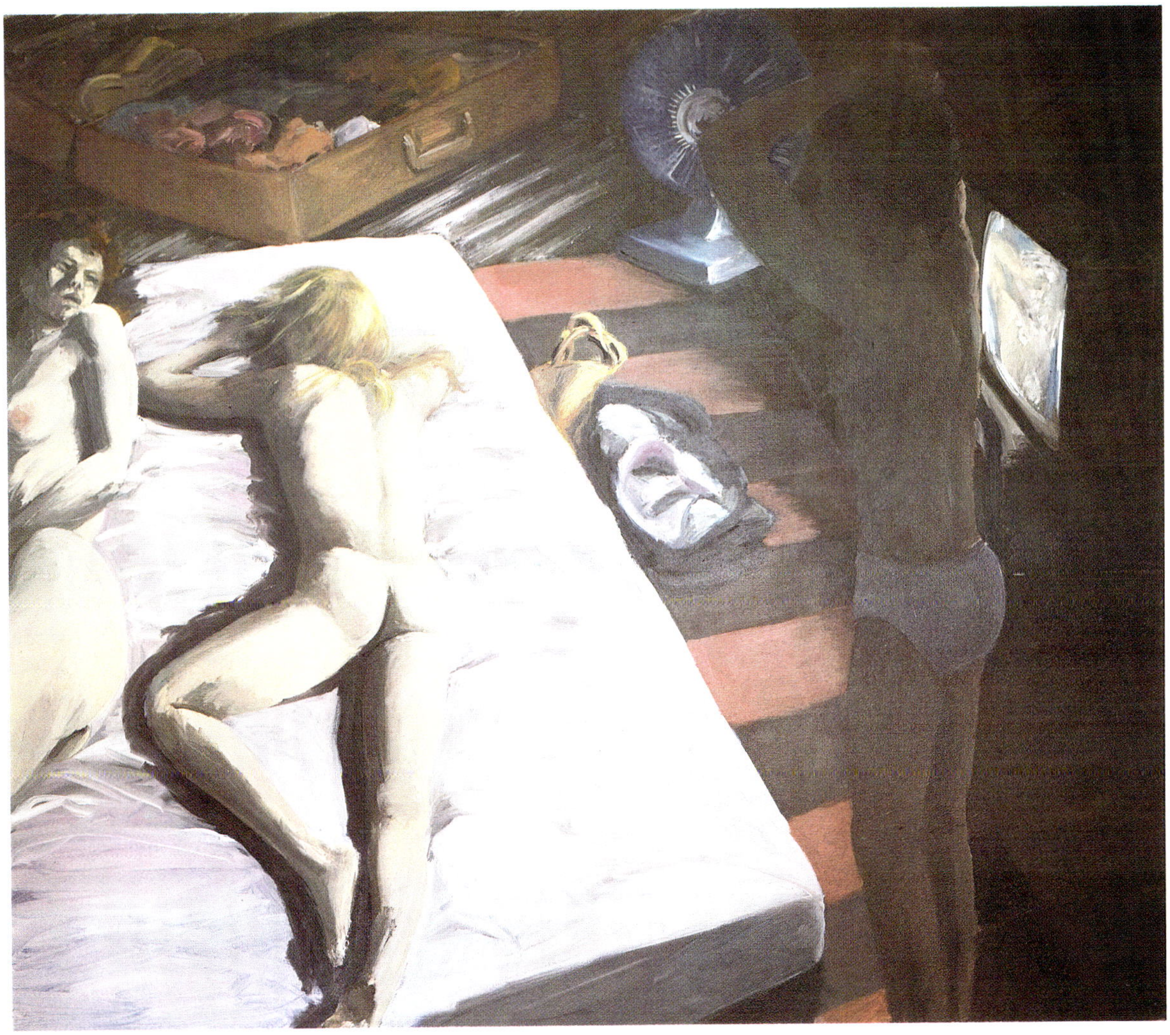

8. *Overnight*
1981
130 x 274
Collection of Mr. and Mrs. Aron B. Katz
New York, New York, U.S.A.

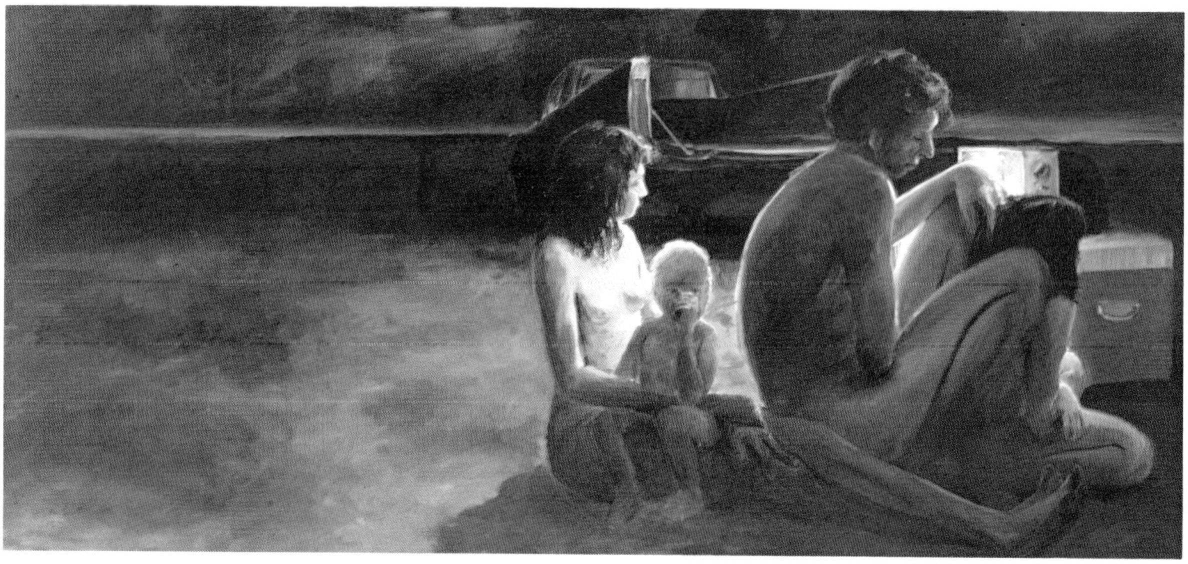

9. *Grief*
1981
140 x 173
Collection of RSM Company
Cincinnati, Ohio, U.S.A.

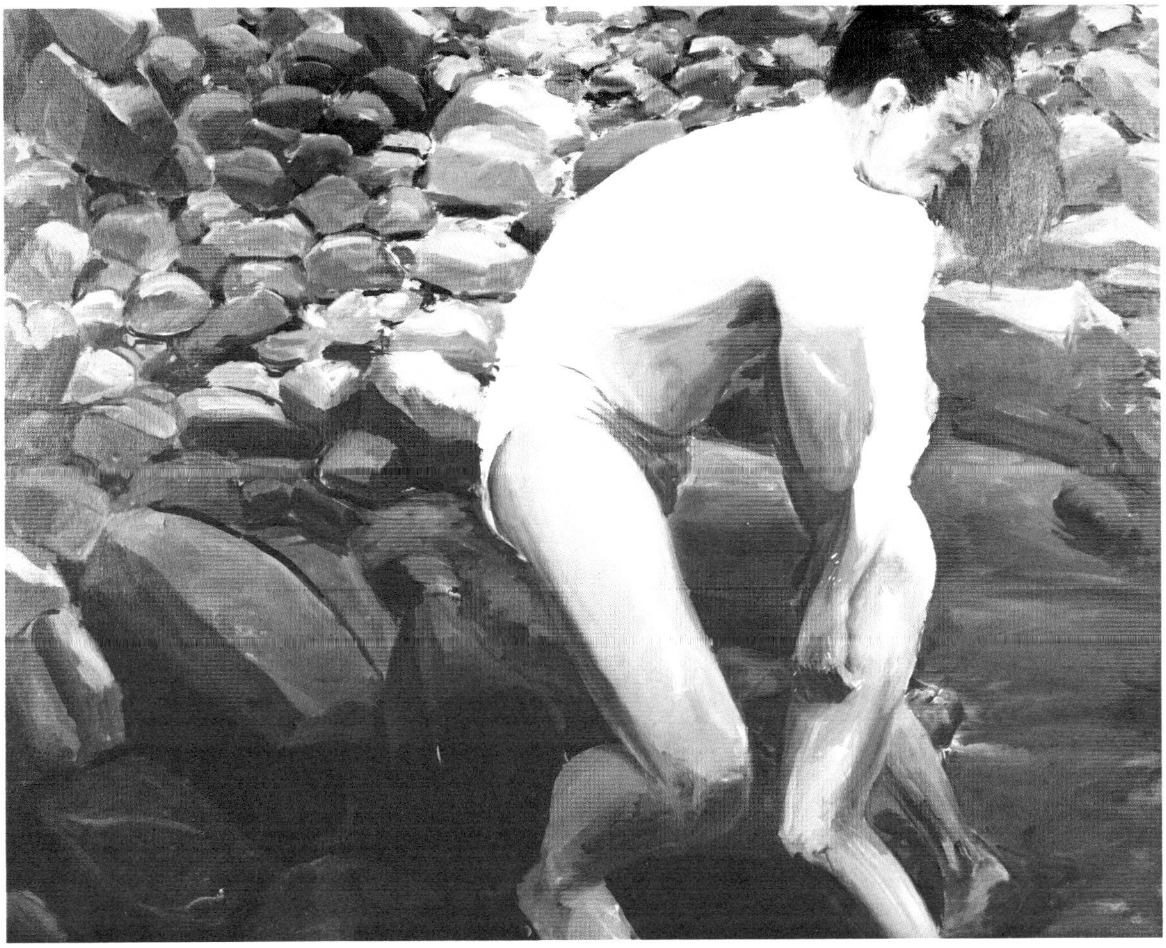

10. *Barbeque*
1982
152 x 254
Collection of Mr. Douglas S. Cramer
Los Angeles, California, U.S.A.

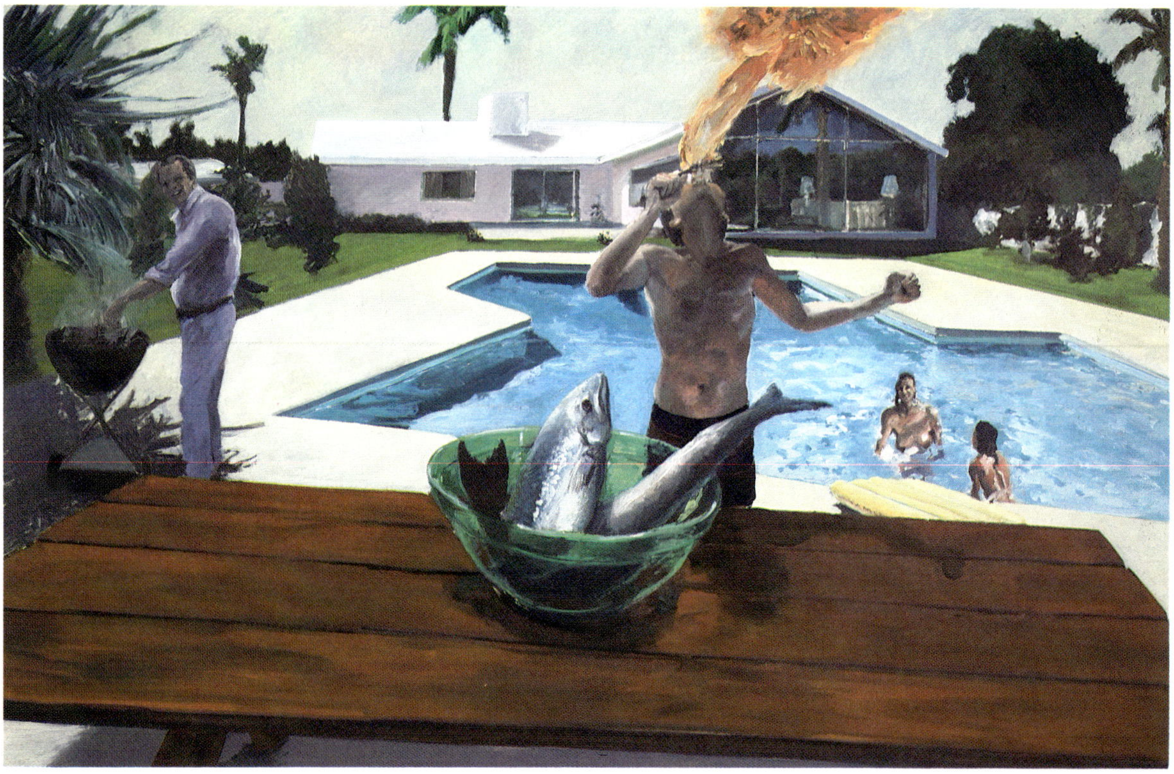

11. *The Old Man's Boat and the Old Man's Dog*
1982
213 x 213
The Saatchi Collection
London, England

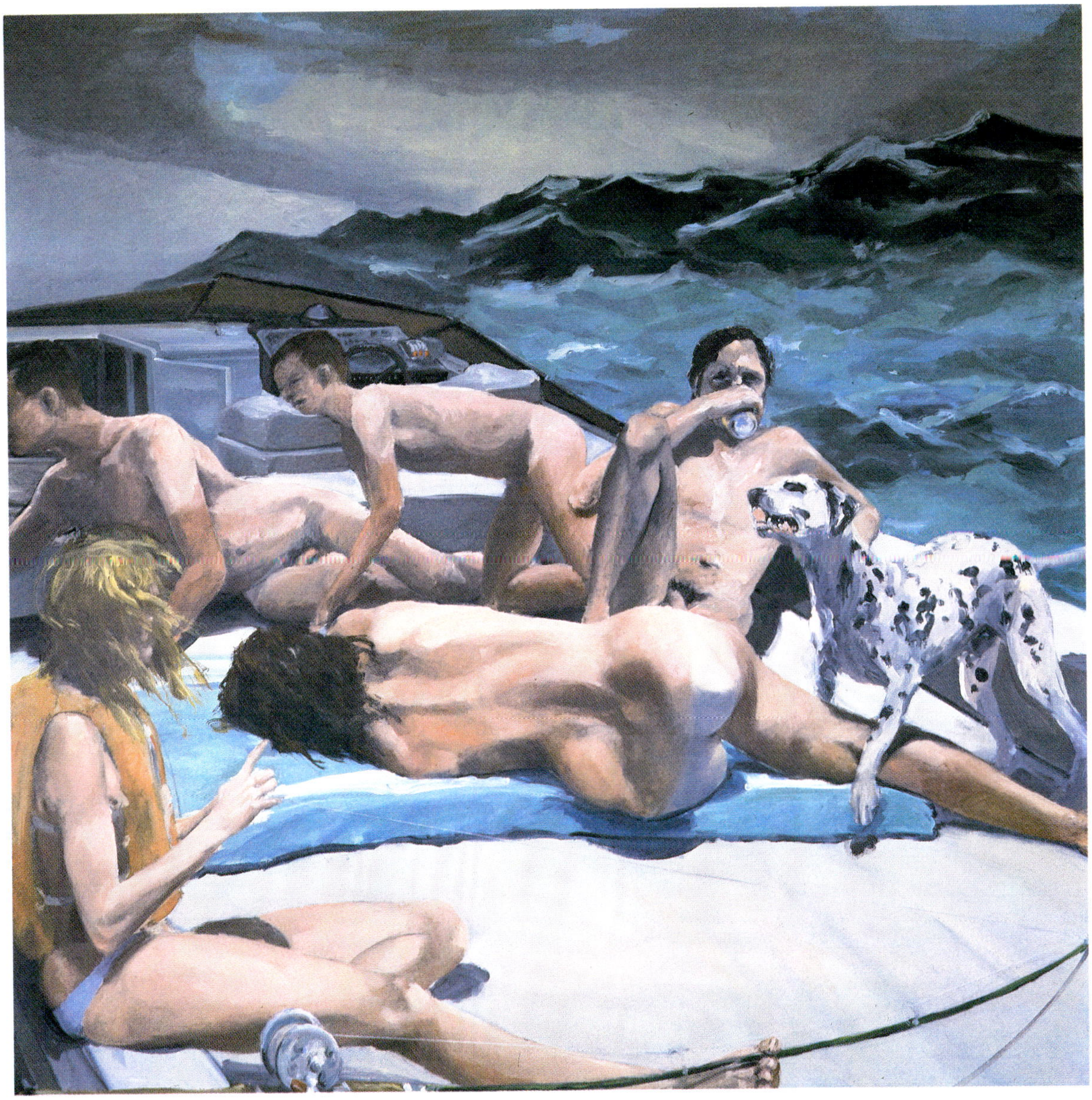

12. *Pizza Eater*
1982
152 x 152
Collection of Lonti Ebers Fine Arts Inc.
Toronto, Ontario, Canada

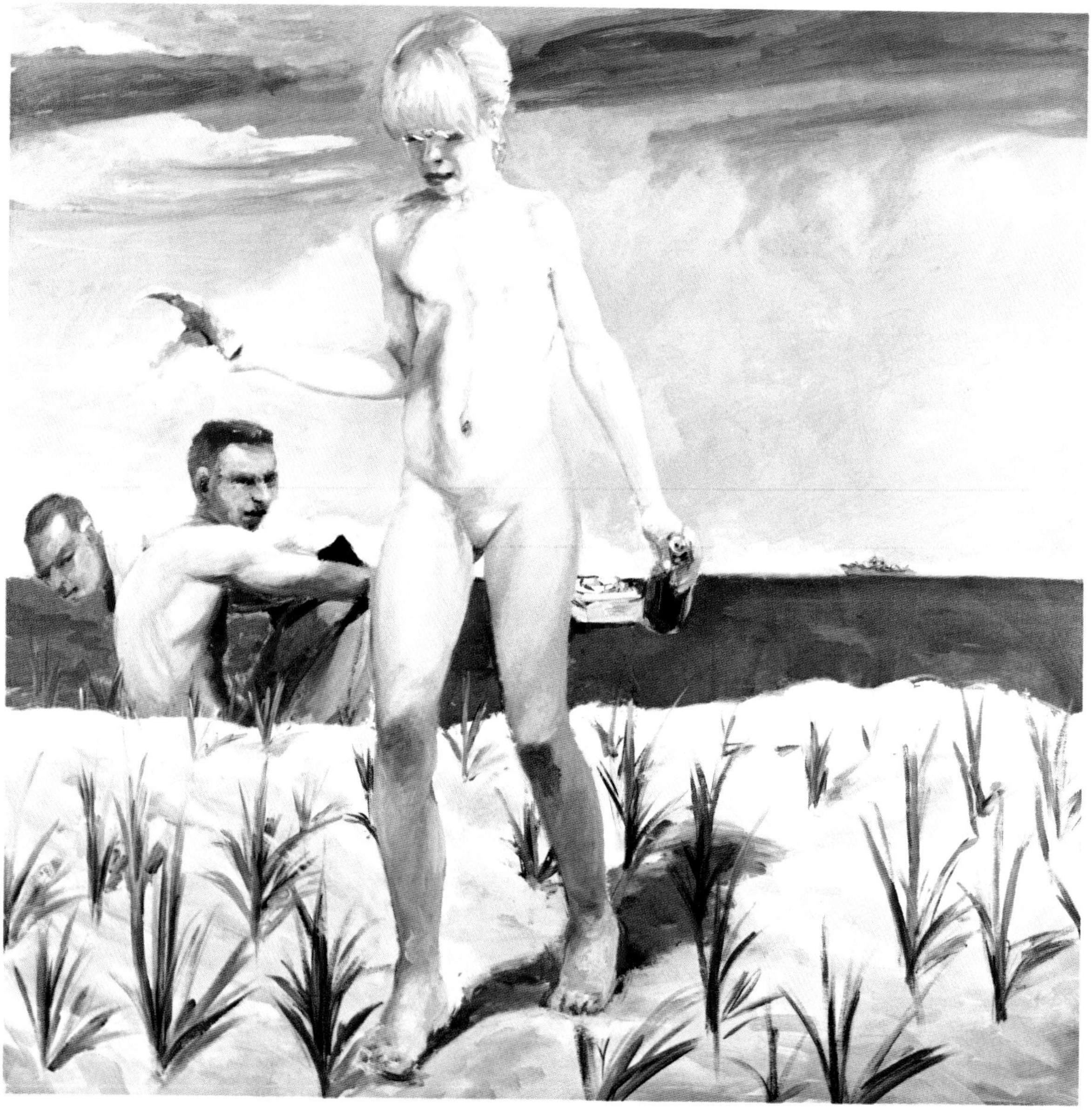

13. *New House*
1982
173 x 244
The Smorgon Family Contemporary
American Art Collection
New York, New York, U.S.A.

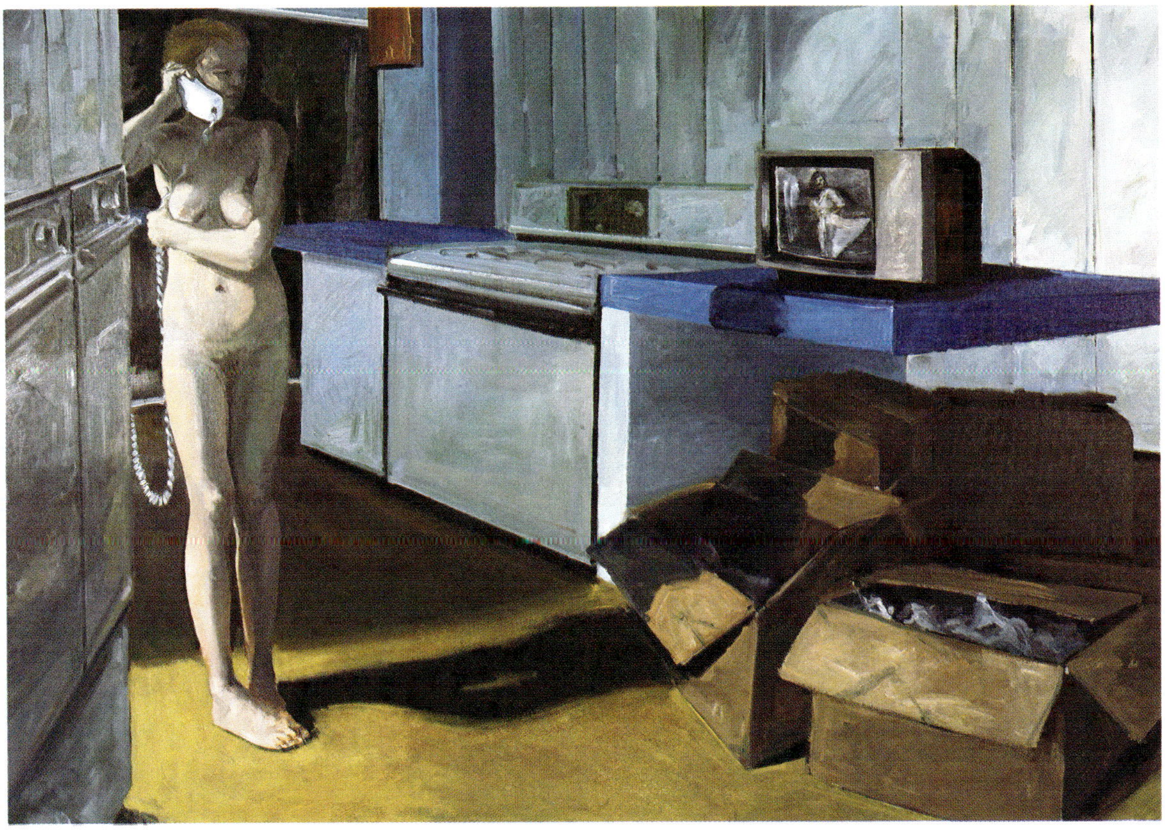

14. *The Sheer Weight of History*
1982
152 x 152
The Downe Collection
New York, New York, U.S.A.

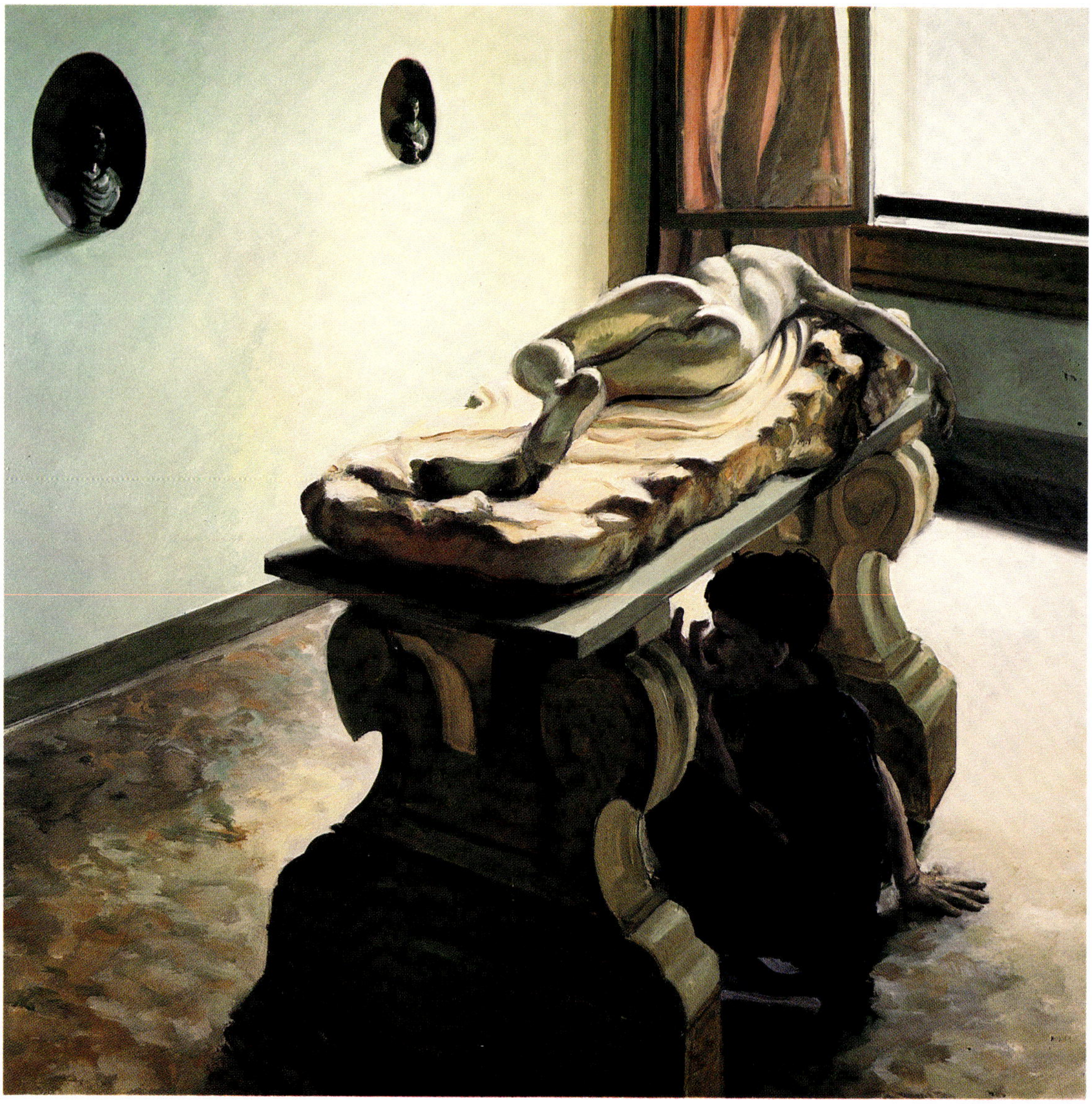

15. *Untitled (Two Women in Bedroom)*
1982
213 x 213
Collection of Lewis and Susan Manilow
Chicago, Illinois, U.S.A.

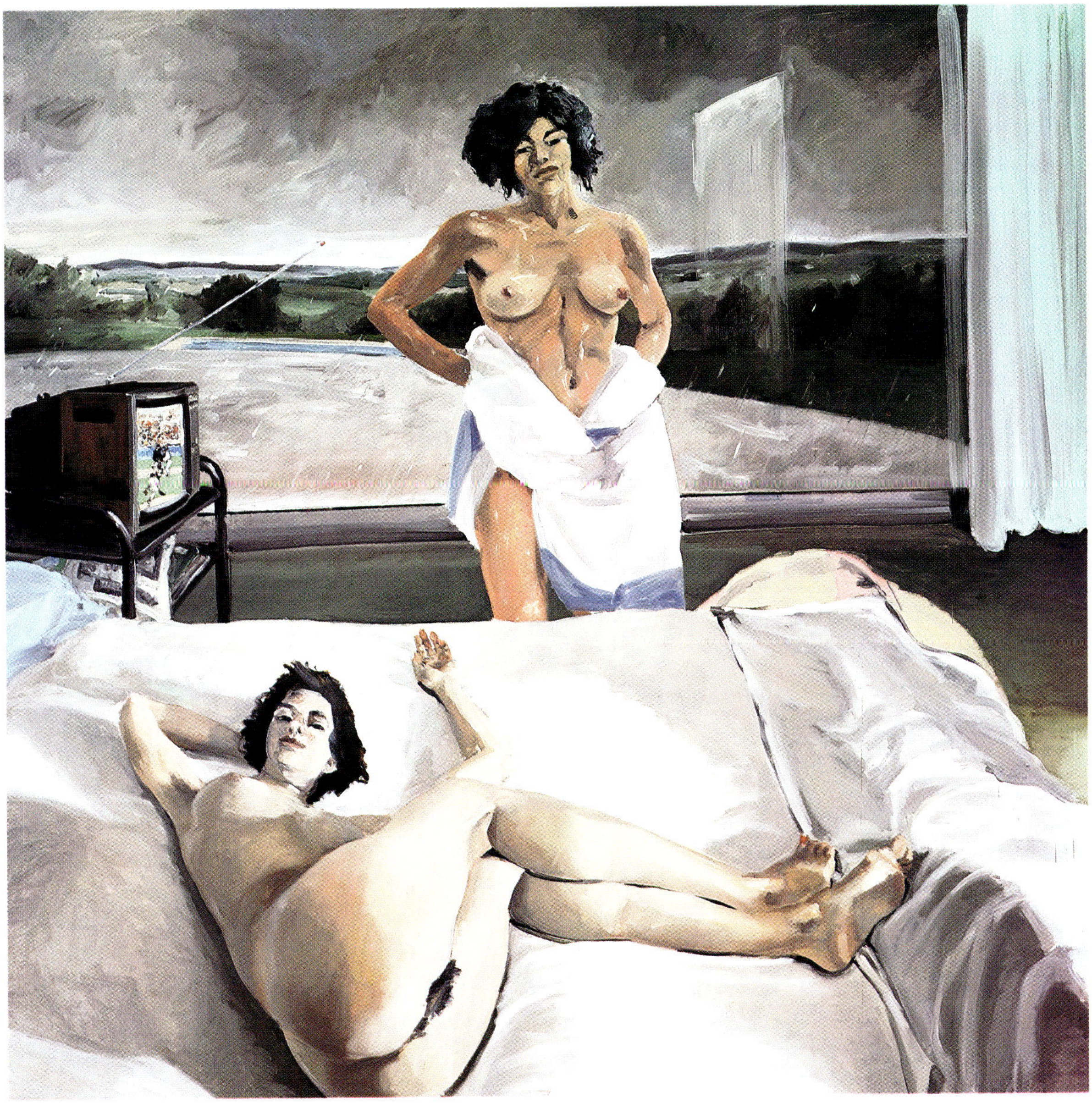

16. *Best Western*
1983
274 x 197
The Speyer Family Collection
New York, New York, U.S.A.

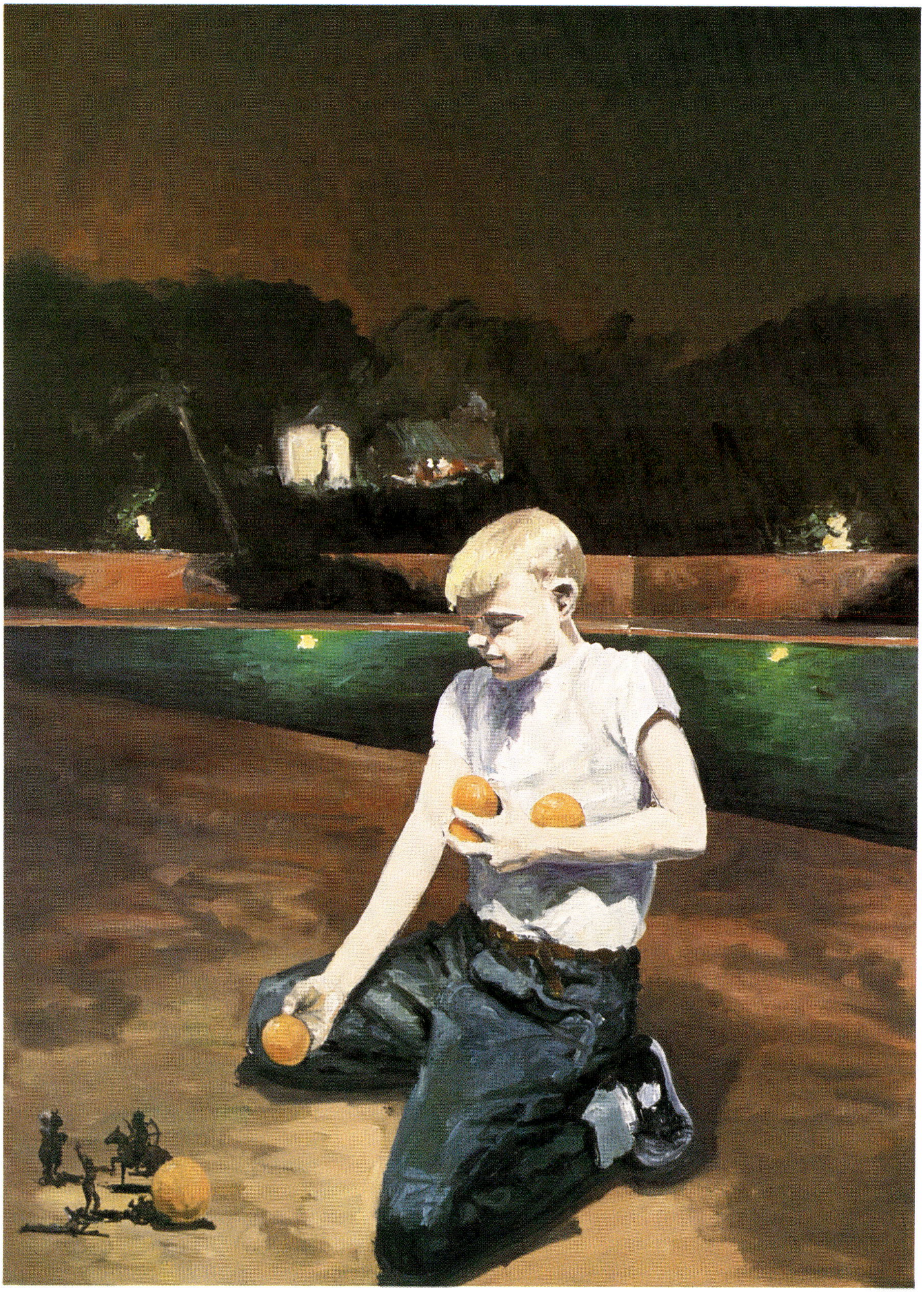

17. *Master Bedroom*
1983
213 x 274
Collection of Mr. Barry Lowen
Los Angeles, California, U.S.A.

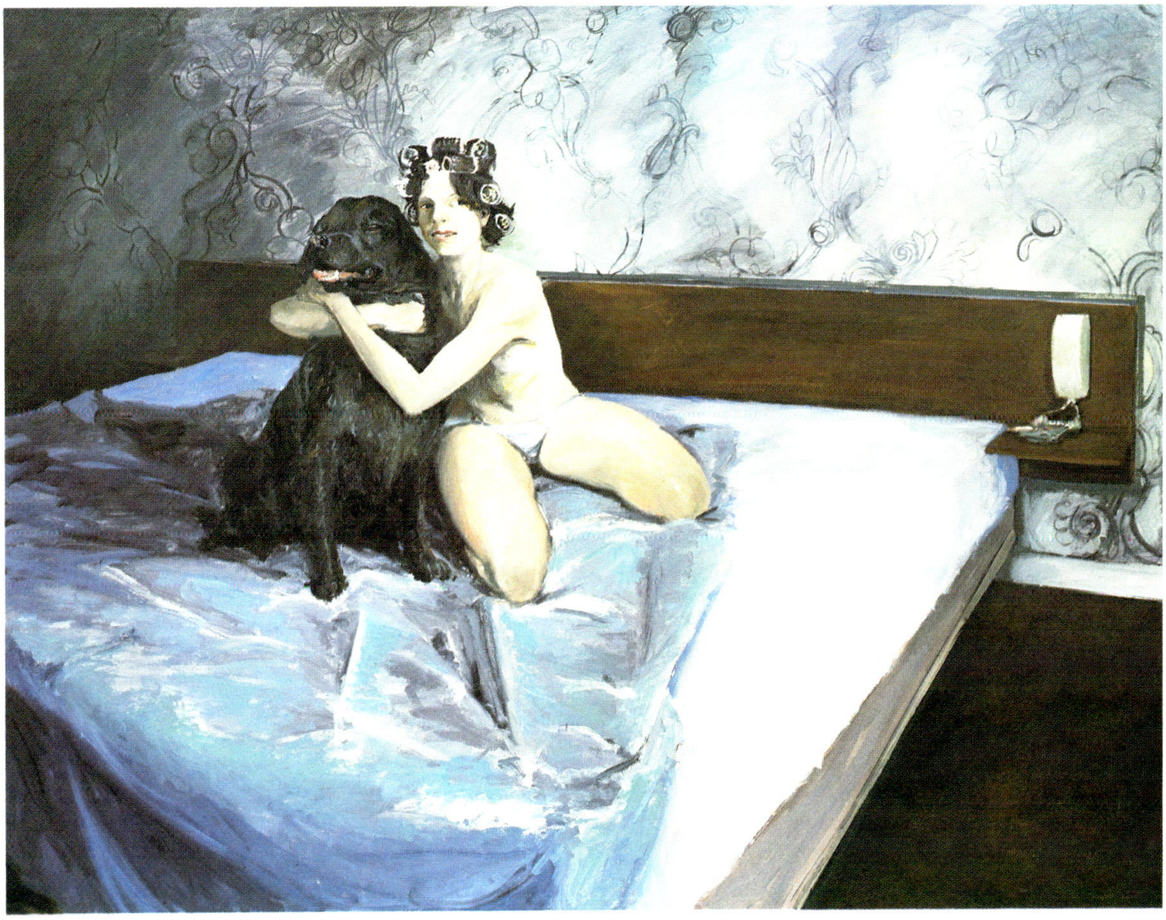

18. *Dog Days*
1983
213 x 427
Collection of Tom and Charlotte Newby
Neenah, Wisconsin, U.S.A.

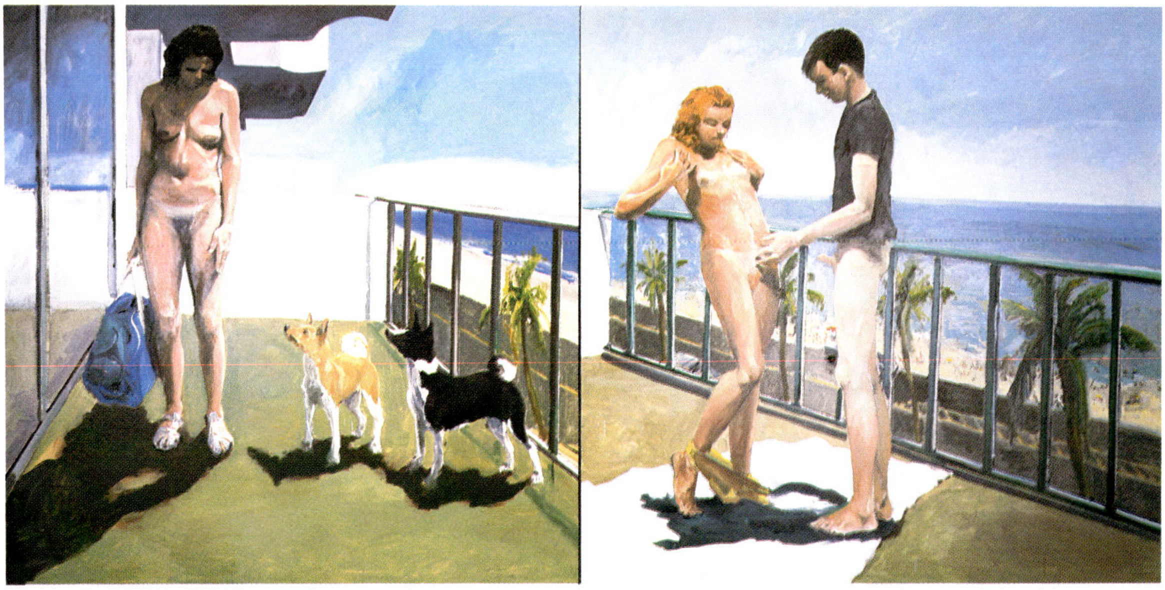

19. *Saviour Mother, Save Your Love(r)*
1984
198 x 274
Collection of The Menil Foundation
Houston, Texas, U.S.A.

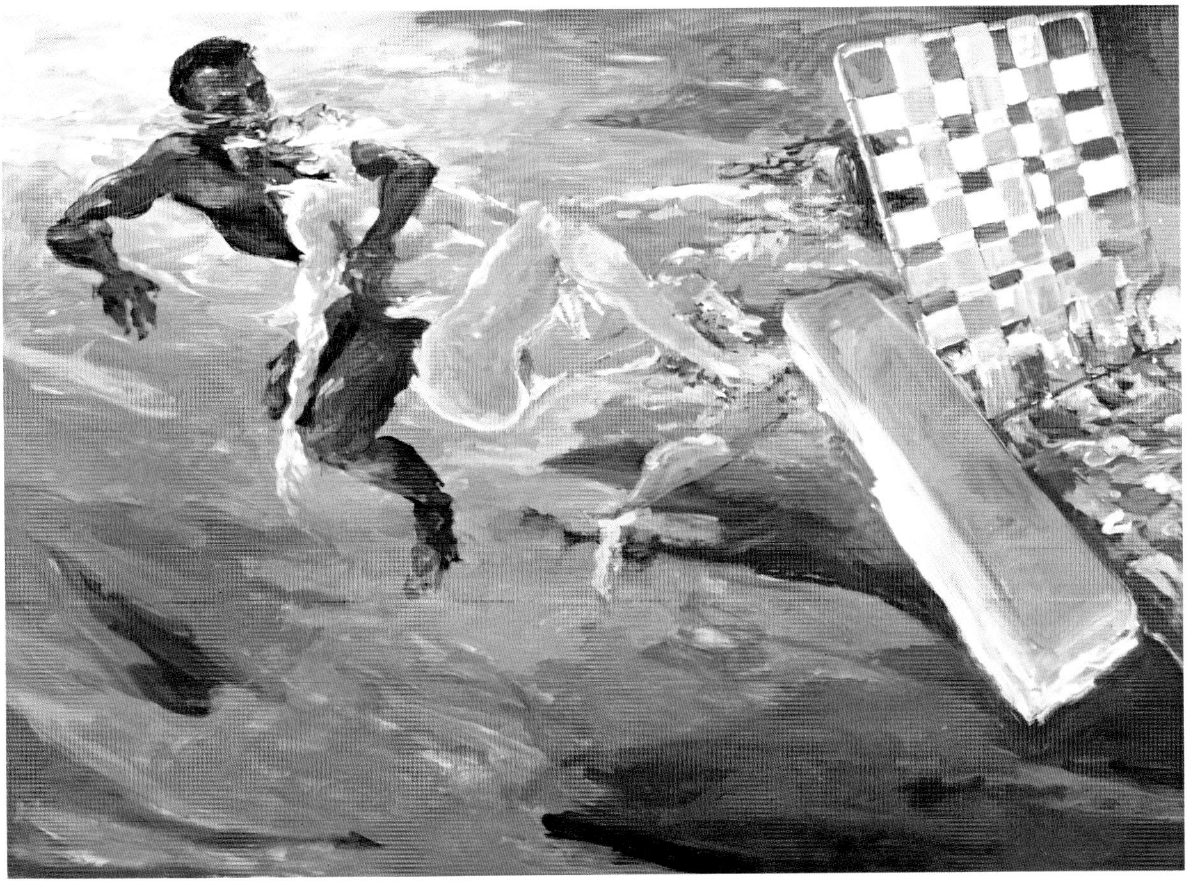

20. *Sisters*
1984
274 x 213
Collection of the artist, courtesy of Mary Boone Gallery
New York, New York, U.S.A.

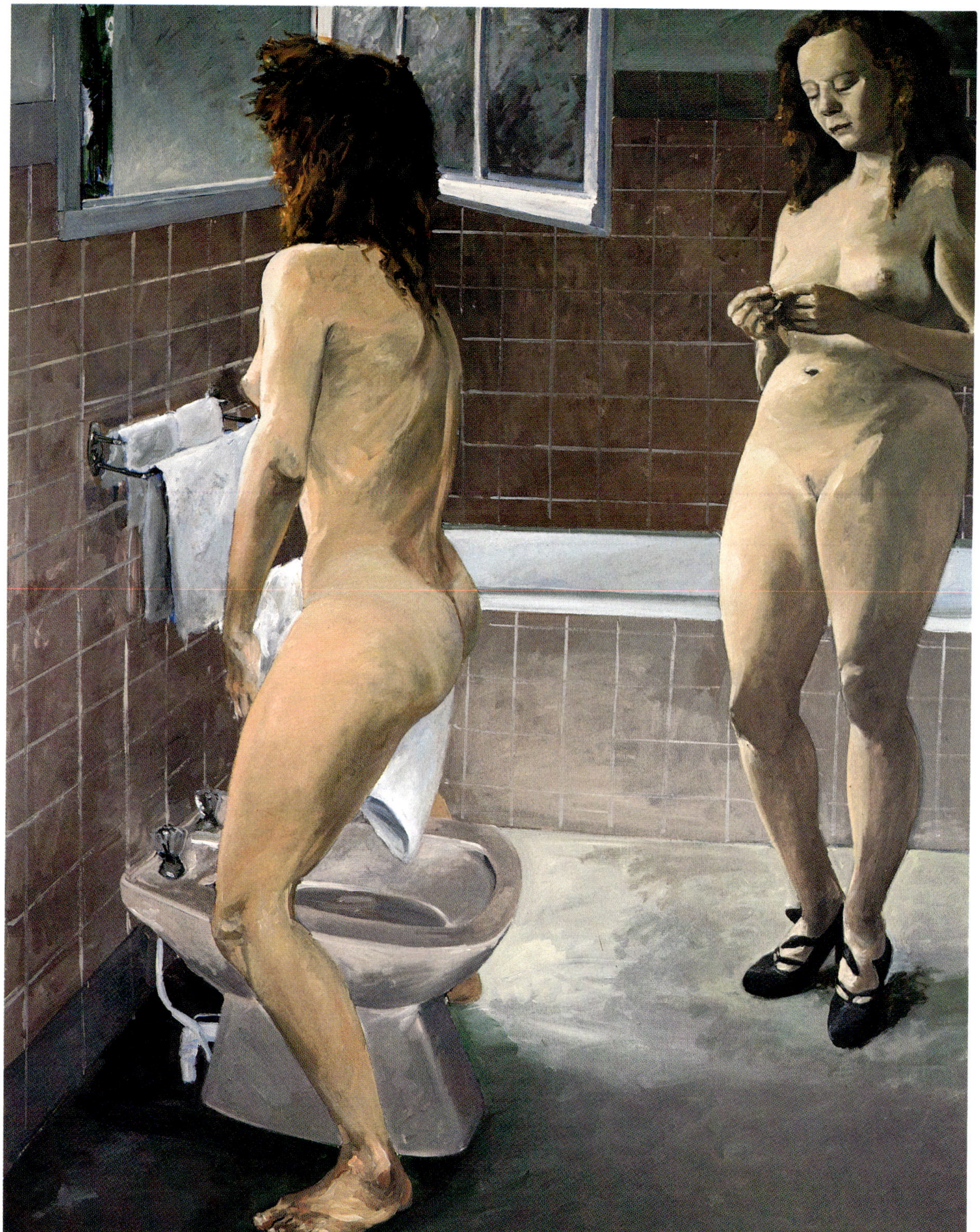

21. *Daddy's Girl*
1984
198 x 274
Collection of Robert and Doris Hillman
New York, New York, U.S.A.

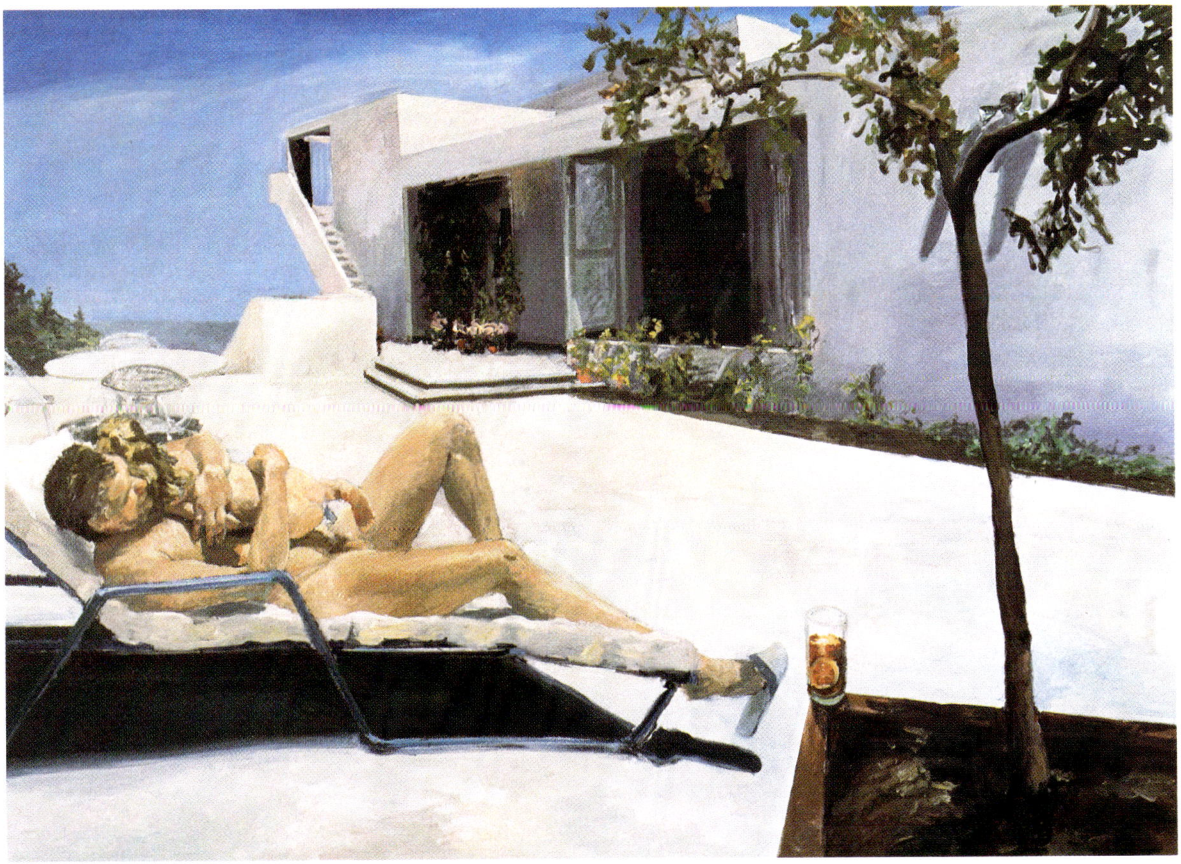

Eric Fischl

1948 Born in New York, New York

1972 Received BFA from California Institute of the Arts, Valencia, California

1974 - 1978 Assistant Professor, Nova Scotia College of Art and Design, Halifax, Nova Scotia

1984 Resides in New York

Solo Exhibitions

1975 Dalhousie Art Gallery, Halifax, Nova Scotia

1976 Galerie B, Montreal, Quebec
Studio, Halifax, Nova Scotia

1978 Galerie B, Montreal, Quebec

1980 Edward Thorp Gallery, New York, New York
Emily H. Davis Art Gallery, University of Akron, Akron, Ohio

1981 Edward Thorp Gallery, New York, New York
Sable-Castelli Gallery, Toronto, Ontario

1982 Edward Thorp Gallery, New York, New York
Sable-Castelli Gallery, Toronto, Ontario
University of Colorado Art Galleries, Boulder, Colorado

1983 Larry Gagosian Gallery, Los Angeles, California
Mario Diacono, Rome, Italy
Multiples/Marian Goodman Inc., New York, New York
Nigel Greenwood Gallery, London, England
Saidye Bronfman Centre, Montreal, Quebec
Sir George Williams Art Galleries, Concordia University, Montreal, Quebec

1984 Mary Boone Gallery, New York, New York.

Group Exhibitions

1975 Time Canada Ltd., Toronto, Ontario, *The Canadian Canvas*

1976 Vancouver Art Gallery, Vancouver, British Columbia, *17 Artists — A Protean View*

1978 Edward Thorp Gallery, New York, New York, *Group Show*
the Gallery/Stratford, Stratford, Ontario, *Coasts, the Sea and Canadian Art*
Kunsthalle Basel, Basel, Switzerland, *Neun Kanadische Künstler*

1979 Edward Thorp Gallery, New York, *Group Show*
Project Studios One, Queens, New York, *The Great Big Drawing Show*

1980 Annina Nosei Gallery, New York, New York, *Drawing Show*
Edward Thorp Gallery, New York, New York, *Group Show*
Glenbow Museum, Calgary, Alberta, *Aspects of Canadian Painting in the Seventies*

1981 Barbara Gladstone Gallery, New York, New York, *Summer Pleasures*
Barbara Toll Fine Arts, New York, New York, *Large Format Drawings*
California Institute of the Arts, Valencia, California, *Alumni Exhibition*
Edward Thorp Gallery, New York, New York, *Group Show*
Museum of Art, Rhode Island School of Design, Providence, Rhode Island, *Art for Your Collection*
Museum of Art, Rhode Island School of Design, Providence, Rhode Island, *New York: Visiting Artists*

Nigel Greenwood Gallery, London, England, *Real Life Magazine*
Robeson Center Gallery, Rutgers University, Newark, New Jersey, *The Reality of Perception*

1982 Barbara Toll Fine Arts, New York, New York, *By the Sea*
College of Art Galleries, Maryland Institute, Baltimore, Maryland, *Drawing: An Exploration of Line*
Edward Thorp Gallery, New York, New York, *Group Show*
Florida State University, Tallahassee, Florida, *New New York*
Josef Gallery, New York, New York, *Narrative Settings*
Milwaukee Museum, Milwaukee, Wisconsin, *New Figuration in America*
Project Studios One, Queens, New York, *Critical Perspectives*
Queens Museum, New York, New York, *Figures of Mystery*
Sidney Janis Gallery, New York, New York, *The Expressionist Image: From Pollock to Today*
Whitney Museum of American Art, New York, New York, *Focus on the Figure: Twenty Years*

1983 Bonnier Gallery, New York, New York, *Small Works*
Castiglioncello-Castello Pasquini, Italy, *Art Itinera 83: Continuing Interest in Painting*
Center Gallery, Bucknell University, Lewisburg, Pennsylvania, *Faces Since the 50s*
Chrysler Museum, Norfolk, Virginia, *Reallegory*
Daniel Weinberg Gallery, Los Angeles, California, *Group Drawing Exhibition*
Edward Thorp Gallery, New York, New York, *Group Show*
Linda Farris Gallery, Seattle, Washington, *Self Portraits*
Mary Boone Gallery, New York, New York, *Paintings*
Parrish Art Museum, Southampton, New York, *The Painterly Figure*
Seibu Museum, Tokyo, Japan, *Mary Boone and Her Artists*
Two PPG Place, Pittsburgh, Pennsylvania, *New York Painting Today*
Whitney Museum of American Art, New York, New York, *1983 Biennial*

1984 Aldrich Museum of Contemporary Art, Ridgefield, Connecticut, *American Neo-Expressionists*
American Pavilion, Biennale Di Venezia, Venice, Italy, *Paradise Lost: Paradise Regained*
Archer M. Huntingdon Art Gallery, College of Fine Arts, The University of Texas at Austin, Austin, Texas, *New American Painting: A Tribute to James and Mari Michener*
Dalhousie Art Gallery, Halifax, Nova Scotia, *The Seventh Dalhousie Drawing Exhibition*
Indianapolis Museum of Art, Indianapolis, Indiana, *Painting and Sculpture Today*
Krannert Art Museum, Champaign, Illinois, *New Painting*
Musee d'art contemporain, Montreal, Quebec, *Via New York*
Palacio de Velasquez, Parque del Retiro, Madrid, Spain, *Tendancies en Neuva York*
Whitney Museum of American Art, New York, New York, *American Art Since 1970*

Bibliography

Ammann, Jean-Christophe. "Zur Ausstellung." In *Kanadische Künstler,* Basel: Kunsthalle Basel, 1978.

Anderson, Alexander and Carrie Rickey. "Up Against the Wall Street: An Investor's Guide to Galleries." *The Village Voice* (October 1980): 15-21.

Balkind, Alvin. *17 Artists - A Protean View.* Vancouver: Vancouver Art Gallery, 1976.

Bass, Ruth. *Art News* 81(September 1982): 176.

——. "New Editions: Eric Fischl." *Art News* 83(March 1984): 82-83.

Becker, Robert. "Art: Creative Coupling." *Interview* (October 1982): 82-85

Berlind, Robert. "Eric Fischl at Thorp." *Art in America* 68(November 1980): 141-143.

——. "Actual Size." In *The 7th Dalhousie Drawing Show,* Halifax: Dalhousie Art Gallery, 1984.

Bogardi, George. "Fischl Explores . . ." *Montreal Star,* 23 March 1978.

Chandler, John. "Seventeen Artists: A Protean View." *artscanada* 33 (October/November 1976): 56-60.

Chandler, Marcus. "Art World: Private Firm Challenges the Stereotype of Art Collecting." *The Indianapolis Star,* 6 February 1983.

Curringer, Bice. "Eric Fischl: Year of the Drowned Dog." In *LOOKS et Tenebrae,* 85-89 (German), 169-173 (English). Zurich/New York: Peter Blum Edition, 1984.

Diacono, Mario. *Eric Fischl: Birthday Boy.* Rome: Mario Diacono Gallery, 1983.

Diehl, Carol. "As Time Goes By." *Art and Auction* (May 1982): 30-32.

Downey, Roger. "Linda Farris' 13th Anniversary Show: Self-Portrait without Self-Revelation." *The Seattle Weekly,* 3 August 1983.

Edinborough, Arnold. "Time Counts the Years . . ." *Financial Post,* 18 January 1975.

Ferguson, Bruce. "In the Middle of a Story/Au Milieu d'une Histoire." In *Eric Fischl: Dessins/Drawings,* Montreal: Centre Saidye Bronfman, 1983.

Fischl, Eric. "Bridge Shield Shelter." In *Eric Fischl,* Halifax: Dalhousie Art Gallery, 1975.

——. "Eric Fischl." In *Kanadische Künstler,* 43-54. Basel: Kunsthalle Basel, 1978.

——. "Picasso: A Symposium." *Art in America* 68(December 1980): 186.

——. "Eric Fischl." *Impressions* (Winter 1982): 9-12.

Friedman, Jon. *Arts Magazine* 56(June 1982): 21.

Glowen, Ron. "Heavyweight Artists Offer Close Look at Themselves." *Everett Herald* (Washington), 5 August 1983.

Greenwood, Michael. "The Canadian Canvas." *artscanada* 32(March 1975): 1-16.

Hackett, Regina. "47 Artists Picture Themselves, Some for Better, Some for Worse." *Seattle Post Intelligencer,* 5 August 1983.

Haskell, Barbara. *Focus on the Figure: Twenty Years.* New York: Whitney Museum of American Art, 1982.